Lurie, Alison.

Familiar spirits.

WITHDRAWN

$22.95

DATE			

Familiar Spirits

✳

Also by Alison Lurie

FICTION

Love and Friendship
The Nowhere City
Imaginary Friends
Real People
The War Between the Tates
Only Children
Foreign Affairs
The Truth About Lorin Jones
The Oxford Book of Modern Fairy Tales (editor)
Women and Ghosts
The Last Resort

NONFICTION

The Language of Clothes
Don't Tell the Grown-Ups

FOR CHILDREN

The Heavenly Zoo
Clever Gretchen and Other Forgotten Folktales
Fabulous Beasts

ALISON LURIE

Familiar Spirits

✳

A MEMOIR OF

James Merrill and David Jackson

✳

VIKING

VIKING

Published by the Penguin Group

Penguin Putnam Inc., 375 Hudson Street, New York, New York 10014, U.S.A.
Penguin Books Ltd, 27 Wrights Lane, London W8 5TZ, England
Penguin Books Australia Ltd, Ringwood, Victoria, Australia
Penguin Books Canada Ltd, 10 Alcorn Avenue, Toronto, Ontario, Canada M4V 3B2
Penguin Books (N.Z.) Ltd, 182–190 Wairau Road, Auckland 10, New Zealand

Penguin Books Ltd, Registered Offices:
Harmondsworth, Middlesex, England

First published in 2001 by Viking Penguin,
a member of Penguin Putnam Inc.

1   3   5   7   9   10   8   6   4   2

LIBRARY OF CONGRESS CATALOGING-IN-PUBLICATION DATA
Lurie, Alison.
Familiar spirits : a memoir of James Merrill and David Jackson / Alison Lurie.
p. cm.
ISBN 0-670-89459-1 (alk. paper)
1. Merrill, James Ingram.   2. Lurie, Alison—Friends and associates.   3. Poets,
American—20th century—Biography.   4. Authors, American—20th century—
Biography.   5. Gay men—United States—Biography.   6. Jackson, David, 1922–
I. Title.
PS3525.E6645 Z774 2001
811'.5409—dc21   00-043594

This book is printed on acid-free paper.

Printed in the United States of America
Set in Bembo
Designed by Nancy Resnick

For Edward

Contents

✳

Familiar Spirits

✳

Foreword

✳

A MEMOIR is a more modest enterprise than a biography. Its author doesn't know and can't know everything: he or she hasn't read all the manuscripts and letters, interviewed friends, or consulted reference sources. A memoir may contain truth, but it cannot be the whole truth. Memory distorts, no matter how hard you try to hang the picture straight. This is so even if one has journals and letters to draw on, as I have—because journals and letters, too, are selective.

What is more, in writing about two friends who played—I think dangerously—with the supernatural, in the shape of a Ouija board, I am in a way playing with my own invisible Ouija board—trying to contact the spirits of the dead. One danger for me, as for them, is that these spirits may speak in my voice and not their own.

✳

In describing this project I have sometimes referred to it as a memoir of James Merrill. People accept this readily, because Jimmy is a famous poet and is dead. But it is also and equally a memoir of David Jackson, who is less well known and not yet dead, though most of his mind is gone.

Indeed David needs a memoir more than Jimmy does, because so few people know who he was or have even heard of him. Bad luck, not lack of talent, ambition, or effort was responsible for this. The world of fame is narrow: it chooses and celebrates only a few. Hundreds, perhaps thousands, of gifted people remain unchosen, unknown.

Sometimes it seems ironic to me that biographers should write of those who have already distilled their own lives into art or into dramatic or heroic acts—people who have left a record. Meanwhile those who have left no record are ignored and forgotten. That is partly why this is a memoir of two friends whom I have lost, rather than one.

Foreword

✳

I should like to thank the friends who have read this book in manuscript and corrected my errors of fact or emphasis, especially Barbara Epstein, Barbara Hersey, Edward Hower, J. D. McClatchy, Phyllis Rose, and Stephen Yenser.

1

Beginnings

✳

WHEN JAMES MERRILL and I first met we didn't take to each other. If someone had told me that day that we would be friends for forty years, I would have thought they were joking.

It was the hot summer of 1950; I and my first husband, Jonathan Bishop, were in Europe on a postponed honeymoon. We had come to Austria to stay with Lynn and Ted Hoffman, who were working at the Salzburg Seminar. An acquaintance from Harvard, Claude Fredericks, was in town, too, and they arranged for all of us to have lunch and go for a swim in a nearby lake. Both

Lynn and I were fond of Claude, and hoped to find the friend he was traveling with, another young poet, equally likable.

But Jimmy Merrill was a disappointment. Compared to Claude he seemed both coolly detached and awkwardly self-conscious. He was thin and pale and short-sighted, with thick black-rimmed spectacles (later he would wear contact lenses). Though only twenty-four, he was clearly already an intellectual and an aesthete. He appeared to have read everything and, worse, to be surprised at our ignorance.

The lake turned out to be a large light-struck shiny pond, mainly surrounded by woods. Fallen tree trunks littered the steep, sandy margin, and more floated offshore. The water was a clear, dark brown, and very deep; a top layer had been warmed by the sun, but below it was icy, and choked with the rubbery yellow and green straps of water weeds.

Most of us splashed about briefly and then waded out, but Jimmy stayed longer; and in spite of his weedy appearance he turned out to be a skilled swimmer. Unlike professional athletes, who often seem to be fighting the water, attacking it with violent slapping assaults and throwing off sprays of liquid shrapnel, Jimmy hardly broke the surface as he swam. The dark wet element parted smoothly for him as it might have for some long, elegant pale fish. When he finally waded out, however, he again seemed chilly and ill at ease.

As his memoir of those years declares in its title, Jimmy was *A Different Person* then, in both senses of the phrase. He was different from most other persons, and he was different from the person he would become. Most of us change as we age, but Jimmy changed more than most. He not only became more confident and better-looking—eventually elegantly handsome—he also became kinder, more generous, and more sympathetic. He never quite became an ordinary person, but his instinctive scorn of fools, once only half-concealed by good manners, relaxed and gave way to a detached, affectionate amusement, such as a highly civilized visitor from another planet might feel. Perhaps that is why he eventually seemed so much at home with the otherworldly beings he and David Jackson contacted through the Ouija board.

※

Jimmy and I might never have met again if we hadn't both found ourselves in Amherst, Massachusetts, five years later. I came in September 1954, as part of the baggage of my first husband, an Amherst College instructor in English. Jimmy, who had graduated from the college in 1947, arrived the following fall as a visiting writer, accompanied by his new friend David Jackson.

In 1955 Jimmy, though less nervous, was still thin and pale, with flat dark hair and something of the air of a clever, inquisitive bird. Later, when I learned that the name "Merrill" could be traced back to the French *merle,* or "blackbird," this seemed appropriate. He no longer casually paraded his superior learning and so-phistication; he had become more sensitive to social situations and able to employ the perfect good manners he had learned as a child from his mother and gov-erness. These good manners were one of his most strik-ing qualities, and they carried over into his work. As he told an interviewer in 1967:

> Manners for me are the touch of nature, . . . Some-one who does not take them seriously is making a serious mistake. . . .
>
> The real triumph of manners in Proust is the ex-treme courtesy towards the reader, the voice explain-ing at once formally and intimately.

By 1955 Jimmy had also become something of a dandy. Though he wore conventional suits and shirts and neckties to official academic occasions, his everyday clothes were elegant but odd, sometimes slightly comic. He had a subtle, rather Art Nouveau color sense: he liked mauve and purple and apricot and turquoise silk or Egyptian-cotton shirts, and bright flowered ties. At home he often cooked breakfast in a Japanese kimono and sandals. I remember especially some red straw and silk sandals and a gray-striped silk kimono with deep sleeves cuffed in black.

At this time Jimmy had not yet achieved the attentive, contained, charming manner of his later years. He fidgeted with things, and was sometimes awkward and uneasy with strangers. He misplaced ordinary objects, and did not know how to drive. He frequently became panicky when faced with a mechanical or practical problem: a broken window blind, frozen pipes, missing student papers, a canceled plane flight.

This, I felt then, was to be expected. I saw Jimmy as a kind of Martian: supernaturally brilliant, detached, quizzical, apart. Naturally he was someone with whom the invisible energies of this world would not cooperate, whom they would trick and confuse. In a sense I was wrong: but in another sense I was deeply right.

Whenever practical things failed, Jimmy's friend David would come to the rescue. He was at ease in the world: he calmed, he coped, he repaired and replaced and reassured. He understood electricity and plumbing and automobile engines. Later, with David's occasionally impatient encouragement, Jimmy would come to manage the practical side of life better. He would own a VW beetle with the license plate POET and drive it skillfully; he would learn to operate a computer, and become a brilliant, inventive cook.

But from the start Jimmy was in stunningly perfect control intellectually. His mind worked faster than that of anyone I'd known: he could answer most questions before you finished asking them. Words for him were like brilliant colored toys, and he could build with them the way gifted children build with Lego blocks, constructing and deconstructing elaborate, original architectural shapes and fantastic machines.

Jimmy also had a gift for making everything relevant. He shared E. M. Forster's belief that one must connect with other people—perhaps only some other people, in his case. If Jimmy liked someone, he would often try to find a bond between this person and himself, a coincidence: he was delighted, for instance, to discover that he and a new acquaintance had stayed in the same pension in Florence, or that I'd been born on September 3, exactly six months later than he.

But what Jimmy connected best wasn't people but words and ideas. He was keenly alert to ambiguity and multiple meanings, and scathingly and inventively alert to banality. Sometimes when I was with him, I would hear a cliché hop out of my mouth, like the frogs and toads that afflict the bad sister in the fairy tale. Usually he would only wince slightly; but now and then he would repeat the cliché in his characteristic drawl, half eastern upper class and half southern. He would play with it in a mild, devastating way, scrutinizing the words with a herpetologist's detachment.

For instance, when I described my six-year-old son's state of mind by saying that he was "as mad as a wet hen," the response was: "Yes. I wonder: would the juvenile equivalent be 'as mad as a wet chicken'? Or perhaps you could use the masculine form, 'as mad as a wet cock.' "

In his writing Jimmy would often casually rescue clichés from banality. In *Sandover*, for instance, he speaks of "this net of loose talk tightening to verse." He was able to give any word or phrase, even the most ordinary, double and triple meanings, connecting it with weather, music, interior decoration, art, literature, myth, history, or several of these at once. A kind of poetic, meaningful punning was one of his specialities. One famous early example is the double pun in "Three Sketches for Europa." The nymph Europa, kidnapped by Jupiter in the shape of a bull, eventually becomes Europe:

11

The god at last indifferent
And she no longer chaste but continent.

Jimmy could make puns in several languages at once: both he and David were fluent in French, German, Italian, and modern Greek, and Jimmy also knew classical Latin and Greek. Most readers and listeners were awed, but a few were made uneasy by the flow of wordplay. One of these dissenters, when I praised Jimmy's verbal wit and skill, remarked, "Uh-huh. A disconnected man, a man without a job or a family or a permanent home, no wonder he's fascinated by connections."

The English Department at that time had only ten members, and they and their wives saw each other often. Even so, Jimmy and I mightn't have become friends if it hadn't been for David Jackson. I liked David instantly—almost everyone did, while it was common back then for people to take time to warm to Jimmy. Because of our bad start in Salzburg, it probably took me longer than most; certainly it was David I loved first.

It's difficult to explain to anyone who only met him later what David Jackson was like in 1955. He was, to start with, wonderfully attractive: blond, tanned, strong. He had grown up in the West, and had the kind of casual, laid-back, wide-open-spaces manner and slow cowboy drawl characteristic of the region. Unlike Jimmy, whose initial reaction to most phenomena was complex and tentative, David seemed easily and warmly interested in everything and everyone. In spite of his down-home manner, he was sophisticated, widely traveled, and multiply talented: at UCLA he had studied music composition with Hindemith and Schoenberg. He wrote and drew and painted and played the piano expertly.

Most of all, David was an acute observer of human behavior. He could see two people glance at each other and guess that they were in love. He noticed when one of my husband's colleagues spoke quietly but unpleasantly to his wife at a party, and that she then rushed into the bathroom and reappeared later smudged with makeup and tears. He pointed out that a certain professor always blinked his eyes several times after he had made a rude remark, as if pretending not to have spoken, or not to have seen its effect.

Sometimes, I discovered later, David's interest in observation led him farther, into what anyone who wasn't a writer might call snooping. He was unashamed of this. "Why should we not exercise our curiosities as freely as other people do their 'manners?' " he wrote me in 1956. "I have never hesitated eavesdropping, peering into letters & diaries—nor do I intend starting to."

In David's published short fiction, and the novels he never found a publisher for, his gifts of observation and deduction were fully in evidence. In real life he usually kept these skills under his hat (most often a worn canvas one with a wide floppy brim), displaying only the casual wit and affectionate concern that made him so popular.

Back then, when homosexuality was less widely accepted, it was to David's advantage that he didn't resemble the stereotype of, as even some enlightened people would have put it, a "pansy" or a "fairy." This was long before thousands of gay men came out of their closets wearing lumberjack mustaches and lumberjack shirts, and worked out in gyms to develop lumberjack muscles. David did not look like a lumberjack, but he looked like a man who had—as he had—been married and fought in Europe in World War II. He dressed casually, in faded khakis and corduroy jackets and white or blue shirts with the sleeves rolled up, and wore old tennis shoes or loafers.

In the 1950s, having been in the army was a source of pride and honor, and there was an invisible line between men who had and hadn't served in the armed forces. It was possible to escape the draft by declaring, in answer to the question, that no, you didn't "like girls"; but this was considered cowardly and shameful. Many young men who could honestly have used this excuse lied in order to serve, as both David and Jimmy did. The lie was always accepted, even when one might have thought it couldn't possibly have been.

✳

Though I had made a few friends in Amherst, I was lonely. My husband, finding himself at twenty-seven the sole support of four people, two of them under the age of three, had become serious, distant, and preoccupied with the need to finish his Ph.D. thesis and hold on to his job. He left the house every weekday morning at 8:30 and returned at 5:30, expecting dinner to be ready and the children quiet and out of the way. In the evenings he read or corrected papers. He also usually spent most of Saturday and Sunday at his office or in the library.

I missed his company, but I also missed Cambridge and the people I'd known there, especially the members of the Poets' Theatre. This was an informal, somewhat disorganized collection of young writers committed to putting on plays in verse: both those of classic authors like Yeats, and ones they wrote themselves. Among them were John Ashbery, Edward Gorey, Frank O'Hara, Donald Hall, V. R. Lang, and Richard Wilbur. Today this list sounds impressive, but in the 1950s all these people were unknown, and the Poets' Theatre was a broken-shoestring operation, mocked in the *Harvard Crimson*, always running over budget and into crisis. Nevertheless it was full of casual excitement, fun, and drama.

Jimmy and David knew some of the members of the Poets' Theatre because by 1955 two of them, John Ashbery and Frank O'Hara, had moved to New York and helped to start another, similar organization called the Artists' Theatre. Jimmy's two verse plays, *The Bait* (1953) and *The Immortal Husband* (1955), had just been produced by the Artists' Theatre. That was one bond between us: the other was that we were all young, practically unknown writers. David and I had published a few short pieces, and we both had a rejected novel or two in our bottom drawer. Three slim collections of Jimmy's poems had appeared, but one was a vanity-press production paid for by his father. (It came out when Jimmy was sixteen and became a lifelong source of embarrassment.) Like the plays, his poetry had created only a shallow though pleasant ripple in the literary world. One of the gifts we gave one another was to read and praise—perhaps sometimes overpraise—one another's work. But overpraise has its uses as well as its dangers. It's possible that without David's and Jimmy's encouragement I might have given up during the ten years in which everything I wrote was rejected. They weren't the only friends who encouraged me to carry on—but they were the only friends who were also writers.

✳

Like most faculty members at Amherst College, we were living in college housing: I and my husband and children in the bottom half of a big, cold white frame house on the Northampton Road, Jimmy and David in a picturesque farmhouse outside of town that belonged to Bill and Nancy Gibson, who were on sabbatical. It has not occurred to me until now that David and Jimmy were probably not only paying more rent than we were, but that they could easily afford it. It was a while, even then, before I realized that Jimmy hadn't come to teach at Amherst for the money, like my husband and his colleagues, but for the fun of it.

In a vague way I gradually gathered that both David's and Jimmy's families were rich, but at first I didn't know how rich they were. I remember the moment I began to understand. David was over at my house, and we were having coffee and cookies. My children, then aged one and three, were napping; and the late-winter sun shimmered through the long, lumpy green icicles that fringed the kitchen window. David was describing the extensive plans he and Jimmy had to travel when summer came, and I said it sounded exciting but awfully expensive. "No, it'll be all right," David reassured me. "We can manage.

"People always think Jimmy's keeping me," he said suddenly, shoving back the flop of dark-blond hair that fell over his square forehead.

Surprised, I said that I'd never thought so. In fact, the question hadn't occurred to me.

"I don't mean you. But I have my own money," David insisted. "People here don't realize. I have forty thousand a year."

"Wow," I said. In 1955 forty thousand seemed an immense sum—over ten times what my husband was currently paid by Amherst College. "That's great."

It was true, David admitted, that Jimmy's income was larger—well, maybe about nine or ten times larger. He didn't mention a figure, but I did the calculation in my head, and the result was off the map.

Jimmy was very rich, it turned out, because he was the son of the Wall Street tycoon Charles Merrill, cofounder of Merrill Lynch. David was moderately rich because his father was a successful southern California businessman. But a financially knowledgeable person, observing Jimmy and David's lifestyle at the time, would have estimated their combined yearly income as well under forty thousand. This suggests, as I believe was the case, that they split expenses, and both of them gave the rest of the money away. Over the many years they were together, they lived in attractive but in no way grand houses in Connecticut, Athens, and Key West. They traveled a lot; but they dressed simply, drove small, inexpensive cars, and did their own shopping and cooking. The only servant they ever had was a cleaning lady.

*

Throughout his life Jimmy spent only a fraction of his income. Much of it went to a nonprofit organization he had set up called the Ingram Merrill Foundation, the name of which reunited his divorced parents, Hellen Ingram and Charles Merrill. The foundation gave grants to writers, artists, and musicians; the choice of grantees was not made by Jimmy alone, but by a four-person board of which he was a member.

He and David also made many individual gifts. My guess is that no one will ever know the extent of their generosity, which tended to be secret—but which often changed lives, including mine. In 1959 they paid for the private printing of my first book, a memoir of one of the founders of the Poets' Theatre, V. R. Lang. A copy of this memoir eventually reached Al Hart, an editor at Macmillan, and he wrote to ask if I had ever written a novel. If there had been no copies of the memoir, it is quite possible that I would never have been published. Luck, and the fact that the computer and desktop printer had not yet been invented, was on my side. If I'd been able to produce the fifteen or twenty copies that friends of my subject wanted, Jimmy and David would never have ordered five hundred from a printer, and many fewer people would have seen the memoir.

As he became better-known, Jimmy was also generous with his time and his words. He signed and donated books, appeared at benefits, read manuscripts, judged contests, recommended other people's poetry. As far as I know, he never refused to comment on a manuscript or provide a blurb for an acquaintance, though some of his comments, read carefully, had a subtly concealed sting in their tail. Manuscripts he didn't wholly like, if he liked or at least tolerated the writer, would be described as "unique," "remarkable," or "an extraordinary achievement"—phrases that pleased the author and publisher but warned off those in the know. "No one but X could have written a book like this" was one of his happiest solutions to the blurb problem.

Occasionally, when I visited Jimmy and David, I would notice some new object that must have cost a good deal—a grand piano, or a wonderful large blurry landscape painting of trees and cows and clouds by their friend Larry Rivers, for instance. But these purchases were infrequent. Most gay men I knew also traveled and bought art, and this seemed reasonable; unlike heterosexual couples, they didn't have to support children and save to send them to college.

I realize now that this lifestyle, far more modest than necessary, must have been a deliberate choice. If they'd wanted to, Jimmy and David could have owned mansions and yachts, expensive cars and Impressionist paintings. They could have joined the international set of rich, famous homosexuals: designers, actors, producers, agents, investors, and men who lived on inherited wealth. That they did not do so was clearly deliberate. Eventually they knew a number of rich and famous gay men, but they saw far less of them than they did of people who were neither rich nor famous nor gay—people like my old tutor, Joe Summers, whom Jimmy had taught with at Bard College, and his wife; Grace Stone, a retired popular novelist, and her daughter Eleanor Perenyi, a journalist and dedicated gardener; and Isabel and Robert Morse, Stonington neighbors.

Amherst in the 1950s was a patriarchal, family-centered society. Men went to work, and women stayed home and took care of the house and children. There were no women on the faculty at Amherst College, and no women students. At faculty parties, the men tended to stand at one side of the room and talk shop, while the women sat at the other side, discussing domestic matters. (It occurs to me now that the reason the men stood up was that they sat down most of the day, reading and writing and having conferences. The women sat down because they had spent most of the day standing up, cooking and cleaning and washing and ironing and shopping and carrying babies and groceries.)

Most of the men at these parties didn't seem to have much to say to the wives of their colleagues, unless they went in for flirtation and seduction. Jimmy and David, by contrast, were happy to speak to us. They also seemed to have lots of free time; they could come to lunch and to tea as well as to dinner parties. And even at dinner they were more apt to talk to me and the other wives, and did not regard subjects like art, interior decoration, clothes, and films as unfit for serious discussion.

In contrast to David and Jimmy, most of the men I met in Amherst seemed solemn and heavy. They were interested in sports and politics, and though they read literature, it was for serious professional reasons, and their reading excluded whatever might seem light or ephemeral. (Most—in some cases all—living women writers, for example, were in this category.) Their recreational interests tended to involve competitive physical exertion, even when no competitor was in sight.

My husband, Jonathan Bishop, for instance, was at this time writing a Ph.D. thesis on Emerson, and was also deeply interested in Thoreau. He was not interested in going for short, slow walks with me or the children, but when not teaching or working on his thesis or correcting papers, he took long, exhausting Thoreau-type hikes in the woods, and up and down the hills around Amherst, where he identified trees, flowers, and birds from guidebooks.

I still vividly recall one warm spring afternoon when, cashing in my baby-sitting credits with another mother, I went to tea with Jimmy and David at their house in the country. They had set a tea table on the lawn, with an embroidered white tablecloth, a silver teapot, sugar bowl, and creamer, flowered china cups, and plates of shortbread cookies and—in honor of *The Importance of Being Earnest*—cucumber sandwiches. In the spirit of the occasion, I had on a flowery, ruffled frock, and David and Jimmy wore pale summery clothes—I especially remember Jimmy's lavender shirt.

Suddenly my husband appeared. He did not walk up the driveway, but smashed and stamped his way out of the thick woods and brush behind us, red-faced and

sweaty, in stained khakis and a dark plaid wool shirt—
and, as Jimmy put it later, recalling the event in a letter,
"plastered with leaves, mud, welts."

No, he didn't want anything to eat, Jonathan insisted:
what he wanted was for me to drive him home, now. I
didn't want to go: I had hardly started to drink my tea.
David and Jimmy, gracefully suppressing their evident
amusement, persuaded Jonathan to sit down and join
us, but only for a few minutes. For the first time in my
marriage, I looked at my husband through their eyes,
and found him both ridiculous and unattractive. The
moment passed, but in a way it was the beginning of an
end that came twenty years later.

＊

When I left Amherst for Los Angeles in the summer of
1957, one of my special regrets was that I wouldn't see
David and Jimmy so often. But we met when I came
back for visits, and more often after I and my husband
and children moved back East in 1961. Meanwhile, so
as not to lose touch, I included Jimmy and David in my
next novel. In the book, which was set in an academic
small town much like Amherst, most of the characters
were intensely involved with themselves and each other.
The character based on David and Jimmy did not play
any important part in the plot; instead he commented

on the action in letters at the end of each chapter. To create him, I put my two friends into an imaginary bowl and stirred, and then divided the batter. What came out was a novelist called Allen Ingram, who was teaching at "Convers College" and writing letters to a painter friend in New York, Francis Noyes. (Allen was the name of the hero of David's current novel, and Ingram was Jimmy's middle name; while Noyes was David's middle name, and Francis the name of the hero of Jimmy's novel, *The Seraglio*.) Like my friends, Allen Ingram represented detachment, worldly sophistication, and ironic sympathy; he was in the book partly to remind the reader that there is a life outside adultery and academia. It occurred to me only recently that my merging of Jimmy and David into a character who contained parts of each was a crude version of the process that may have created the spirits of the Ouija board.

2

Journeys

✳

THE 1950S AND EARLY 1960S were a good time for
David and Jimmy. They were young and in love; they
had no economic worries; they lived in an odd but
beautiful house in a picturesque village on the New England coast. When not at home they traveled together
round the world and made friends everywhere.

Except for the church spires, 107 Water Street, Stonington, Connecticut, was the tallest structure in town, a
brown-shingled box four stories high with a wide view
of the sea and sky from its top floors. It had been built
as a commercial block, and after they bought the building Jimmy and David continued to rent out the shops

on the ground floor and the offices just above. Gradually they transformed the upper floors into two apartments. The smaller one faced north and contained a guest bedroom, kitchen, and bath. The larger became an exotic duplex, with kitchen, sitting room, study, and two bedrooms on the third floor, and stairs to a big black-and-white-tiled music room and sundeck above.

Jimmy's study in Stonington, like later ones in Greece and Key West, was very small—formerly, in fact, a closet—with a shelf desk and many bookcases, some displaying a small art object or postcard. He sat in a straight wooden chair with a flattened cushion. Even after he owned a computer he wrote in longhand, often on half sheets of paper or the backs of letters. There were many drafts piled on his narrow desk, many notes and fragments; yet each slip of paper, no matter how small or torn, gave the impression of an almost Oriental, calligraphic elegance. There were no smudges or blots; long, graceful, flexibly curved arrows indicated where a new word or phrase went; lithe slashes crossed out rejected lines. Sometimes the pieces of paper looked handmade, like thin crinkled silk or thick, creamy parchment.

In 1960, tired of climbing three steep flights of stairs with luggage or groceries, David and Jimmy installed a tiny elevator. It was lined in bamboo and silvered rice paper; its cushioned bench was covered with a blue-and-white Japanese print.

＊

I visited Jimmy and David often in Stonington from 1956 on, usually alone but twice, awkwardly, with a child or two. That wasn't a good idea: the place wasn't designed for children, and contained too many fragile objects. Jimmy liked to tell the story of how, after he had reprimanded my oldest son, John, then four, for temporarily locking him out on the sundeck, John turned to me and cried, "I don't like that man, and I'm never going to say that anything he has is beautiful again."

As even a four-year-old could see, 107 Water Street was beautiful. The rooms were full of light and air, the tables heaped with flowers and picture books and magazines. The sitting room window that faced Water Street had a border of alternating red, blue, and orange glass panes that transformed the houses and boats and clouds outside and fascinated my children. Everywhere were the trophies of David and Jimmy's trips abroad: Indian statuettes, Japanese netsuke, Tibetan hangings, and Persian miniatures; a nineteenth-century silhouette from England, a tiny ancient jade dragon from China. Each object was usually strange in some way: the dancing Indian gods had elephant heads and many arms; an eighteenth-century fan, when opened in one direction, showed flowering trees, but in the other direction it revealed a pornographic sketch in faded brown ink.

I loved visiting Stonington. To go to 107 Water Street from a house cluttered with shabby, worn furniture and toys and dirty laundry and the cries of children was like being transported to another world: one not only more attractive, but more luxurious, calm, and voluptuous; more free and leisured—a world in which the highest goods were friendship, pleasure, and art.

In Stonington, and later in Greece and Key West, David and Jimmy were perfect hosts: suggesting all kinds of entertainment, but never demanding that their guests partake of it. And Jimmy was becoming a gifted and original cook. He could invent amazing meals out of leftovers, and was especially brilliant at desserts: chocolate and coffee mousse, apricot tart, local blackberries simmered in brandy and poured over vanilla ice cream.

As a chef, Jimmy was by turns extravagant and economical. Sometimes he would buy expensive French wine and raspberries out of season; but he also saved everything and used up leftovers. It was he who taught me to make stock from the remains of the chicken we had just had for dinner—including the bones and vegetables left on our plates. Now, whenever I do this, I see him in his Stonington kitchen, with its view of stars or blowing treetops. He wears a navy-blue canvas apron and is chopping an onion and a couple of carrots to add to the stock, while he gossips about the guests who have just left.

Skilled as he was in the kitchen, Jimmy at this time was still uneasy when it came to household repairs. When a pipe leaked or a wall socket spit sparks, he panicked. David, on the other hand, took that sort of thing calmly. He knew where the fuse box was, and the main tap. When he couldn't fix something himself, he was superb at dealing with plumbers, carpenters, electricians, and building inspectors. While Jimmy hovered awkwardly or hid in his study, David was friendly, knowledgeable, and laid-back.

Often at dinner there were other guests, some staying in the building and others who had rented or owned summer houses in Stonington. At David and Jimmy's I met Elizabeth Bishop (a faded, very pretty woman in a pale-blue cardigan sweater, who spoke with shy enthusiasm about the books she was reading). Also John Cage and Merce Cunningham, who both seemed to be amazingly tall and thin, and whose conversation, as I remember it, was mainly about Japanese gardens and finding and cooking wild and psychedelic mushrooms.

One summer Truman Capote took a house in Stonington and saw Jimmy and David constantly. I met him first on the beach: a very small semihuman figure in brief bathing trunks, with great dark eyes and damp lank blond hair, halfway between Ariel and Silenus—a classical sprite and a little fat man. It was too cold to swim for long that afternoon, so after splashing about for a while we all sat in a row on damp towels, looking at the water and the passing boats. Then Truman stood up and cried in his piping, unworldly voice, "Come on, Alison. Let's run." I didn't want to run, but such was the force of his personality that I rose, took the plump but strong little hand he held out, and trotted along the gritty sand. "Isn't this fun?" he asked. But I couldn't agree; I could see that Jimmy and David were trying not to laugh, and felt myself to be part of a peculiar, uneasy spectacle.

Truman did not return the following summer. Soon, when he began to move in more expensive circles, he dropped Jimmy and David and began referring to Stonington as "Creepyville."

David and Jimmy's life, as I saw it in Stonington and New York, and later in Athens, and as it was reported to me in letters, was more exciting and varied than my own. They traveled extensively, lived in interesting places, and met unusual and amusing people.

In 1956–57 they visited the Far East; in 1959 they spent months in Europe, reporting their adventures to me in letters and postcards from Japan, India, Denmark, France, Germany, Italy, and Portugal. They went with introductions, and were generously received and feted. In Venice, for instance:

> There was a Masque given us in Peggy [Guggenheim]'s garden. Alan Ansen wrote it and four others plus Alan in a blond string wig and draperies (as Venice) did it, and a snickering audience, with PG, JM, and I on thrones wearing wreaths, listened. (Letter from David, August 1959)

Jimmy's impressions of new places tended to be aesthetic, with an emphasis on the visual and verbal. From Japan, for instance, he reported:

> Language problem severe. As soon as one's companion starts not understanding he produces a sound ef-

32

fect we have come to recognize, a kind of muted, wispy wail, whose "tone" might be defined as hovering between (among) deprecation, incredulity and alarm. . . .

We dashed to a temple, Kiyomizu, to get the cobwebs out of our ears: fine view off high wooden terrace into a mossy valley, rock, fern, maple (all the trees have such small leaves, it seems, like Altdorfer forests), the tints just beginning, water plashing, and the whole scene so littered with wet paper and cardboard that D. first took it for tastefully arranged stonework. Gradually I come to understand what is meant by natural beauties: this country breeds the eye down to small scenes, landscapes made out of food, even. (October 23, 1956)

David's letters, on the other hand, tended to focus on the social world. He was also far more aware of—and angry about—inequality and injustice. In January of 1957 he wrote from India:

The country is, after all, one continuous ruin of civilization after another—and absolutely the most vexing poverty one has ever seen, or dreaded to

see. . . . Scabby diseases, skeletons, beggars, mud vil-
lages, mangy, boney dogs and rags . . . Only the
crows are fat, and increasing in numbers. They are
like the government officials and the *rich* Indians
slopping around in gold-threaded saris, speaking
Oxford English, full of metaphysical ideas and talk
about Beethoven. (January 6, 1957)

And a year later, from Santa Fe:

I guess you gathered we had NYear's Eve in New
Orleans? Segregation prevailed and only the Whites,
us Whites, crowded through the Latin Quarter blowing whistles. It took us a day to get over that. (January 1958)

As time passed, some of David's social awareness
rubbed off on Jimmy, but not a great deal. Occasionally
he would joke about this. "We all have our limits," he
declared in a 1967 interview. "I draw the line at politics
or hippies." And a year later he told Ashley Brown, "I
guess I'm an arch-conservative. More arch than conservative, I'm sometimes made to feel." Politics also frightened him, as he admitted in one of his most famous
poems:

Journeys

I rarely buy a newspaper, or vote.
To do so, I have learned, is to invite
The tread of a stone guest within my house.

Gradually, though, Jimmy's intellectual elitism began to dissolve, and he became sympathetic to a much wider range of people and situations. At the same time David began to take more pleasure in the refinements of landscape, art, and literature.

✳

Even when they were home in Stonington David and Jimmy's life was usually amusing and varied. They were open to new experiences—though sometimes surprised by the results:

I am writing you in the semi-dark [David reported from Stonington in June 1958]. There are only two candles burning. JM is stretched out on the couch, his hands over his eyes, having eaten 8½ illusion-producing mushrooms . . . (dry as dust) which came from Mexico, that interior region where they discovered, not long ago, a mushroom-eating cult. Within four hours he is supposed to have some visions. I ate two and had such trouble swallowing them I've decided to write you instead, glancing up from time to time checking reactions (from what I can see of them in this gloom). . . .

NEXT DAY
No effects from mushrooms. For a moment, there, things seemed to be happening: "I saw a lilac bush turn into a chandelier!" But nothing more happened. Perhaps it's not the season for visions. (June 9, 1958)

They gave impromptu parties, and put on amateur concerts and theatricals. In August 1960, for instance, David described "the second in Stonington's One World Festivals":

We are doing The Wasteland with six voices, a piano, bass fiddle, drums, zyther (Robert Morse) and bells . . . tonight's program will end with . . . 18 haiku poems set to 4-bar jazz rhythms.

They played literary games, one of which involved setting Proust to the tune of the *River Kwai* march. "Here is my first effort," Jimmy wrote:

Journeys

Swann's Way, a book by Marcel Proust,
Tells how the hero took to roost
Racy
Odette de Crecy
Who to his friends could not be introduced

Howard Moss tried his hand:

"Wednesday" said Mme. Verdurin,
Ready to serve her dreadful flan.
Morel
has had a quarrel
With Baron Charlus for using Man-Tan.

And Bernie Winebaum introduced a smutty note
we had been trying to keep out:

Francoise, why must I go to bed?
I'd rather play with girls instead.
Later
I'll have a waiter
But only after my grandmother's dead.
  (March 1960)

It was, I often thought, the happiest marriage I knew.
Jimmy and David were nicer to each other than most

husbands and wives, more affectionate and considerate. They clearly loved each other and preferred each other's company to that of anyone else. And this commitment was imagined as lifelong, or even more. Later, when one of the spirits they contacted through a Ouija board offered them brilliant but separate reincarnations, Jimmy protested indignantly:

> Ephraim, this cannot be borne. We live
> Together. . . .
> Now tell me, what conceivable delight
> Lies for either of us in the prospect
> Of an eternity without the other?

Jimmy and David also seemed more alike, better suited than most husbands and wives. Both in a way lived sideways to life, observant, detached, enjoying the world's variety. They were connoisseurs of cities, languages, landscapes, people. Of course, as a friend once pointed out when I said this, they didn't have the problems of most other marriages: uncertain careers, crying babies, cross teenagers, difficult in-laws, not enough money. They could live wherever they liked, buy whatever they wanted.

On the other hand, David and Jimmy were both men, and the world did not support their sort of happy marriage. Instead, many people scorned and ridiculed it, or worse. Their union was not celebrated in magazines and films and popular songs, approved by relatives, and legitimized by the state. No outside pressures kept them together, as it did so many of us—only the internal magnetic force of their own love.

And agreeable and colorful as their lives usually were, there were gray patches. Occasionally, especially in the winter, when many of their friends' houses were empty and shut, Stonington could seem boring:

> We sit up here and give dinners to people and have others on weekends and play bridge and the piano and, sometimes, the typewriter. Less often the latter. (Letter from David, November 8, 1959)

It was at times like this, especially, that they were apt to turn to the Ouija board, and supplement their overfamiliar human visitors with new and thrilling supernatural ones.

3

Fame and Failure

✳

IN THESE EARLY YEARS, the contrast between Jimmy's and David's professional careers was still not yet pronounced. By 1959 Jimmy had published a short novel, *The Seraglio*, and another brilliant collection of poems, *The Country of a Thousand Years of Peace*. Eight of these poems were addressed to David. Most of them celebrate their love, but one, "Dream and Waking," memorably recalls a quarrel and reconciliation and suggests what the strains in the relationship were:

> . . . for a wild
> Half-hour the light burned, the clock ticked.

You called me cold, I said you were a child.
I said we must respect
Each other's solitude. You smiled.

Well, I shall wake you now,
Smiling myself to hide my fear. . . .

            your slow eyes
Which meet mine, fill with things
We do not name, then fill with the sunrise
And close, because too much light stings.

Already Jimmy guessed what might come, and come between them. I discovered this myself one summer morning in Stonington when David was out shopping. Jimmy was making lunch, and we were discussing a current literary scandal. He remarked that it was better not to have affairs with famous people, because then you found that you didn't become their friend.

"I've never had an affair with a famous person," I said a little regretfully, leaning against the kitchen counter and eating a sprig of parsley.

"Well, I have," Jimmy said, separating lettuce into crisp bite-sized leaves. "And now I don't know them anymore. But the famous people I didn't have affairs with I still know."

I wanted to ask for names, but didn't think I had the right. "You know, Jimmy," I told him instead, half as a joke and half as a compliment, "one day you will be a famous person." I expected him to laugh and protest, but I was wrong.

"Yes," he said, slicing a ripe red tomato with his little serrated knife. "I know it."

❊

David, by the summer of 1959, had written and almost succeeded in publishing three novels. There were many heartbreaking near misses: in 1956, for instance, he wrote me to say that the British publisher Chatto & Windus had almost accepted his latest manuscript:

> You would hardly recognize poor old *Amy* after my last revision of her, so cleaned up, so to the point, so much *trying* to be loved . . . well, that swinish outfit voted 3–2 against; even Day Lewis' nice letter swearing by the book failed to make India seem wonderful that bleak day. Oh, what will we do, dear fellow-sufferer? (January 6, 1957)

In September of 1957 another British publisher, André Deutsch, declared that it wanted the book, but in the end nothing came of that either.

David, refusing to be discouraged, began a fourth novel. Two years later he was still sending this manuscript around, and had started a fifth. He still had great hopes for success, and these hopes were warmly encouraged by Jimmy, one of whose most lovable qualities was his steady, enthusiastic belief in his friends' work.

I believed in David's work, too. I knew he was at least as talented as I, and his novels, which were loosely based on his own experiences in Colorado, California, and Europe, were full of wonderful passages, both comic and serious, and seemed likely to appeal to a wide audience. The description of places and people was perceptive, the dialogue vivid, the plots dramatic and convincing as long as they involved family relationships, conflicts over money and property, and the experiences of people caught up in war and history.

Only the love stories sometimes rang false, and I thought I knew why. Always, as he planned a book, David turned half his male characters into unconvincing females. Once when I suggested that this might be a mistake, he explained that he didn't want to write homosexual novels, which would at best reach only a small audience; he wanted to be read by everyone, everywhere. (In defense of David's decision, it should be said that at that time there were few or no gay bookshops and very little gay fiction on sale. Most homosexuals were in closets, from which they seldom dared to emerge and buy a book about people like themselves.)

David's dreams of success were in some ways more ambitious than Jimmy's. Jimmy knew—we all knew—that his work, however many prizes he won, would always reach a limited audience. The great American public does not read much poetry, certainly not the sort of complex, literary verse Jimmy wrote. He was content with this, and remained so. When in 1983 David Kalstone, in an interview, asked Jimmy if he wouldn't like a larger audience, his answer was: "When I search my heart, no, not really. . . . Think what one has to *do* to get a mass audience. I'd rather have one perfect reader."

Like David, I was beginning to doubt that I would ever make it as a writer. The most I dared hope for was that one of my books would be published, however obscurely. I half-believed my husband's verdict, that I had merely a very minor, shallow talent, and was simply wasting my time putting one word after another. After all, by the spring of 1961 I had published nothing for ten years except the memoir of V. R. Lang that Jimmy and David had paid to have printed. I was beginning to feel the situation was hopeless, and was blown away when, because a friend's brother liked the memoir and sent a copy to his editor, I found a New York publisher for my third novel.

David and Jimmy were full of congratulations, and we all took it as a sign that David's turn would come soon. And why not? He had just published a fine story, "The English Gardens," about two American poets in Munich. One, an attractive young man called Meredith, has much in common with Jimmy. The other, Nicholas, is a former juvenile delinquent who has adopted the role of tough beat poet as a low-effort profession; in appearance and manner he strongly suggests Gregory Corso. The story appeared in *Partisan Review* in May 1961 and was later chosen for the 1962 O'Henry Prize collection.

Yet as time passed, David's turn did not come. He continued to send out his manuscripts, but rejection followed rejection. After a while he began to slow down, to write less often:

I am not working [he wrote in November 1962], I have done five pastels of rooms and of JM and myself, a new substitute for work. I cannot even run a typewriter with anything like my old efficiency.

And when David did work, neither he nor Jimmy was enthusiastic about the result. In January 1964 he wrote:

> JM says the s/s [short story] I've just finished is Bru-
> tal Banality, or Brutally Banal I guess he said. It is.
> And my novel, 6 chapts underway, is a Hopeless
> Farce.

But over the next couple of years David continued to have productive periods, and in 1964 he completed a fine short novel based on his experiences as a young soldier in occupied Berlin, *Pigeon Vole*. The main characters were exotic and fascinating: a Russian major, an anti-Nazi German industrialist, and a beautiful cabaret singer. In a way it was a kind of historical sequel to Isherwood's *Berlin Stories*, and worthy of comparison with that book. But *Pigeon Vole*, too, failed to find a publisher; it was privately printed in 1966.

*

As David began to despair under the weight of accumulated rejection, travel became more and more of an escape for him. Almost every year he and Jimmy went abroad, more and more often to Greece. Late in 1964 they bought a house on a hill in Athens and began to spend the winter months there.

The house is total heaven [Jimmy wrote], you can't believe how pretty, with a view of boundless pines ascending to a tiny white monastery. Balconies, tout confort, heat, sofas, and all, all ours. (October 2, 1964)

Forty-four Athinaion Efivon, though charming, was even more modest than the apartment in Stonington. Jimmy wrote in a tiny former laundry room built on the roof terrace, haunted, as he put it, by "ghosts of dirty / Linen," with one window and a doorway he had to stoop to enter.

That first winter they returned to America in January, and in the spring term of 1965 David taught a writing course at Connecticut College, which—although he complained about grading papers—he much enjoyed. Yet the attraction of Athens was too great, and he refused to teach in America again. Meanwhile Jimmy came back fairly often for readings and lectures, and in the spring of 1967 for a term as writer-in-residence at the University of Wisconsin.

Athens had many advantages over Stonington. It was warmer in the winter, and socially and artistically lively. Also, the growing disparity between Jimmy's and David's reputations was nearly invisible in Athens, since neither of them was published there. They learned modern Greek, explored the country, and traveled to the Greek islands; they made many friends and found young lovers.

They also renewed their interest in the Ouija board, which had amused and entertained them in the 1950s, and now would provide the material for *The Book of Ephraim*. They took it up again casually at first; as Jimmy put it in September 1965, "We rang up Ephraim the other day—1st time in 4 years." But later the sessions with the spirits became more serious. Ephraim's lighthearted and amusing messages began to be replaced by solemn, complex metaphysical lessons from greater supernatural beings. As time passed, the Ouija board would consume more and more of their time—and, it seems possible, more and more of David's frustrated creative energy.

✳

By the time I visited them in March 1975 Jimmy and David were becoming disenchanted with Greece, and there was an undercurrent of scorn and impatience in their descriptions of the local tourist sights. Jimmy's young boyfriend, Strato, was growing up; he would soon be of an age to marry and raise a family. David's boyfriend, George, who was in the Greek merchant marine, was already a man in appearance. I met George one night at a bar: he was handsome and tough-looking, with black hair and eyes and a restless manner, no longer a puppy or a pet as in the photos I had seen. Clearly he was tired of that role, and perhaps tired of David. He drank one beer after another, and when the dancing started, he shouted and stamped with the other grown men, ignoring David's requests that he return to our table.

A few days later David took me on an overnight tour to Delphi and Corinth. Even before we left Athens it became clear that something was seriously wrong. It was very hot, and David, who had always been a casual, competent driver, was now consumed with road rage. He cursed any car that went too slowly or too fast, so violently that I began to wonder if it was me he hated. When another driver tried to pass, he refused to give way. He growled and hunched his shoulders inside his white T-shirt, which was beginning to show damp gray patches, shook his damp blond hair back from his face, and smoked one Greek cigarette after another.

Outside the car David's impatient anger continued: he objected to the restaurant where we stopped for lunch, and rushed me through the gift shop, declaring that everything there was made in East Asia (he may have been right). At Delphi he wanted to leave almost as soon as we arrived. I wanted to stay: the steep rocky hill, the wisps of smoke rising from the grottoes beneath the weedy piles of stones, seemed a place where I might learn the truth. What's the matter with David, what's the matter with me? I wanted to ask, but it was centuries too late.

On the way to Corinth David took what he said was a shortcut, and soon we were driving up a dusty, barren mountain on a road that became narrower and narrower and then turned into a stony goat track. In spite of my fears, David refused to turn back; he jolted along the track and eventually down the other side of the mountain, round precipitous washed-out curves. He wants to die, I thought, as we skirted a cliff on which were gray, warped olive trees and a herd of gray, skinny goats, but I don't, not yet.

※

David's last published work reflected the disappointment with Athens that both he and Jimmy were beginning to feel. It was a long, witty, erudite review of two books on Lord Byron's Greece that appeared in the June 10, 1976, issue of the *New York Review*, and struck a cynical tone about local myth-making.

> The Orwellian rewrite of a struggle against oppression is nearly complete in today's Greece. So many

stops have been pulled out, gloriously by Byron, rather blindly by Shelley, and quite irresponsibly by Leigh Hunt and others, that Greece as helpless Sacrifice to the Bloodthirsty Turk is an image forever imprinted on the public mind.

4

The Ouija Board

✳

> . . . the crack in the tea-cup opens
> A lane to the land of the dead.
>
> —W. H. Auden

JIMMY AND HIS OLD SCHOOL FRIEND, the novelist Frederick Buechner, had played with a Ouija board casually in 1953. But his and David's real involvement began one slow hot August evening in Stonington in 1955, still just as a lark; they had no idea then of how high and how far this lark would fly, or what a monstrous bird of prey it would finally become. They didn't suspect that what started as an evening's amusement would consume so much of their lives over the years to come, or how at times it would become so absorbing that reality itself would seem faded, flimsy, and ghostlike.

The Ouija Board

*

Devices for encouraging messages from gods and spirits (or, according to another view, from one's own unconscious) are very old: they can be traced as far back as Egypt and ancient Greece. In the mid-nineteenth century a contraption called a planchette became popular in Europe and America. This was a small heart-shaped board supported on two wheels and holding a pencil. When the planchette was placed on a sheet of paper, it occasionally wrote legible words; at other times it just sat there or produced meaningless scribbles.

In 1899 a small businessman called William Fuld improved on this device, creating what he called "OUIJA, the MYSTIFYING ORACLE." At this period the Near East was considered the source of everything magical and exotic, and the name "Ouija" sounded vaguely Arabic. But in fact it was merely a combination of the words for "yes" in French *(oui)* and German *(ja)*. Fuld's invention was, literally, a YesYes Board—appropriately so, since what it promised was essentially affirmation of the operator's hopes and fears.

Though Ouija boards were available commercially from 1902 on, they did not become widely popular in America until World War I, when many people wanted to contact friends and relatives who had died in battle or been reported missing. From then on, sales were steady, increasing during and just after World War II, and then again in the 1970s along with the vogue for all sorts of New Age and mystical merchandise.

Today Ouija boards are everywhere. There are nearly two million current messages about the device on the Internet, along with invitations to buy not only the object itself but a dozen how-to-do-it books and tapes. Several currently famous spirit mediums began their contact with the other world through the Ouija board, and—judging from a sample of Internet postings—there is hardly an American teenager who hasn't experimented with it, perhaps as a result of the same sort of impulse that leads them to explore reputedly haunted houses.

The Ouija board is a simple contrivance: a piece of heavy white cardboard about eighteen inches high and twenty-four inches wide, printed with the letters of the alphabet, the numbers from 1 to 0, the words YES and NO, and the symbol &. To consult it, most inquirers today employ a plastic triangular pointer that glides easily on three felt-tipped feet. The seekers sit opposite each other or (more often) side by side, and each places one hand lightly on the pointer. If they are lucky (or, possibly, unlucky), it will presently begin to move of its own accord, spelling out messages from the spirit world.

The Ouija Board

※

In Stonington Jimmy and David consulted the Ouija board in the third-story tower room of their house, an octagonal cupola adjoining the sitting room, painted vermilion pink inside with white Victorian trim, and lit by five windows. They sat side by side at a round table with a white milk-glass top, on Victorian chairs painted lavender. The board in front of them was of the standard pattern, but instead of the commercial pointer they used an upside-down blue-and-white willowware teacup; its handle indicated the letters. When they traveled they sometimes took along a homemade folding Ouija board, with the letters and numbers marked on heavy paper.

At first, as is usual in such cases, nothing happened. But after a while, as Jimmy describes it in *The Book of Ephraim*, there were indeterminate motions:

> The cup twitched in its sleep. "Is someone there?"
> We whispered, fingers light on Willowware,
> When the thing moved.

The early messages were confusing and incoherent. Later on the spirits explained to David and Jimmy that these communications should be disregarded—they came from confused and inarticulate recently dead entities. The first legible message—ominous or moving or both, in the light of what was to come, was: "HELLP O SAV ME." The suggestion was that someone unknown was in great danger, perhaps even—because of the word hidden in the misspelling—in danger of damnation.

At this point, Jimmy "slumped," apparently ready to give up. David, however, said, "One more try" and asked, "Was anybody there?" Suddenly "YES a new and urgent power YES / Seized the cup" and words began to pour forth. They were being contacted, it turned out, by one Ephraim, "A Greek Jew / Born AD 8 at XANTHOS," a favorite of the Emperor Tiberius. Jimmy and David were excited, enthralled, but not wholly surprised. As David told their friend the poet and critic J. D. McClatchy in 1978:

> Everything is interesting when you're that young. Our lives were young together and I think the feeling was that no miracles would surprise you, when you're in love. . . . So it didn't seem really very astonishing that miracles happened.

At first, because of the limitations of the Ouija board, its communications resembled unpunctuated telegrams. But after a while, with the "concurrence" of

Ephraim, David and Jimmy augmented the board's alphabet with ten punctuation marks, including ? and !.
As a result, messages from beyond began to look a little
more like ordinary prose, though they were still always
recorded in the capital letters printed on the board.
Also, at Ephraim's suggestion, Jimmy and David propped
a mirror in a facing chair: "We saw each other in it. He
saw us."

＊

In the beginning both David and Jimmy treated the
supernatural revelations with a light, uncritical humor;
Jimmy remarking later in *Ephraim* that, after all, the
point

> Was never to forego, in favor of
> Plain dull proof, the marvelous nightly pudding.

As time passed, they would consume more and more of
this marvelous pudding, even after they could see that it
was beginning to replace the daily bread of reality.

> —This outside world, our fictive darkness more
> And more belittles to a safety door
> Left open onto light. Too small, too far
> To help. The blind bright spot of where we are.

Later still the safety door sometimes seems to have closed entirely. At one point, after their second spirit guide, Mirabell, has told Jimmy and David that "WE & YOU MOVE IN OUR FIELD TOGETHER" and called them "OUR LOVED ONES," Jimmy, wholly entranced, replies:

> Dear Mirabell, words fail us. How banal
> Our lives would be, how shrunken, but for you.

5

Sandover

✳

IN THE MID-1970S, after over twenty years of off-and-on communication with the spirits of the Ouija board, Jimmy decided to use their revelations as the source of a novel more traditional than any he had yet written: its narrative "limpid, unfragmented," its "characters, conventional stock figures." The basic story would be "The incarnation and withdrawal of / A god." But the project did not go well:

> The more I struggled to be plain, the more
> Mannerism hobbled me. What for?

Since it had never truly fit, why wear
The shoe of prose? In verse the feet went bare.

Presently he lost the manuscript of this novel, leaving it in a taxi when on the way to visit his friend Stephen Yenser in Los Angeles. Instead of trying to rewrite the novel he began a long poem that would use the same material more directly, describing the result as:

The Book of a Thousand and One Evenings Spent
With David Jackson at the Ouija Board
In Touch with Ephraim Our Familiar Spirit.

The Book of Ephraim appeared in 1976. It was followed by *Mirabell* (1978) and *Scripts for the Pageant* (1980), both also based on messages received from the Ouija board, and adding up to a 560-page epic poem in which, instead of conventional stock figures, a whole company of gods and angels and demons and ghosts appeared. The three volumes were finally published together in 1982, with a *Coda: The Higher Keys*, as *The Changing Light at Sandover*.

Some readers and critics have considered *Sandover* Jimmy's greatest work, comparing it to Yeats's *A Vision*, Blake's prophetic books, and Dante's *Divine Comedy*.

Others have been baffled and disappointed. I enjoyed and admired *Ephraim*, but when the subsequent parts appeared, I didn't read them very carefully; after a few pages, I began skipping the messages from the spirits and concentrating on the poetry. By this time I was both bored and made uneasy by the Ouija board, and I politely disregarded it the way we disregard those of our close friends' enthusiasms that we do not share: Indonesian music, for instance, professional football, or crossword puzzles. Only when I decided to write this memoir did I read the book through.

Essentially, Jimmy decided to follow the example of Dante, Blake, and other classic writers; to create a long, ambitious, serious poem dealing with complex philosophical issues. He began it with some reluctance, as he suggested in a Class Day talk at Amherst in 1980. Speaking of the impulse that led poets like Eliot or Pound to attempt a monumental work, he said in *Recitative*:

These men began by writing small, controllable, . . . poems. As time went on, though, through their ambitious reading, their thinking, their critical pronouncements, a kind of vacuum charged with expectation, if not with dread, took shape around them, asking to be filled with grander stuff. . . . I speak, alas, from experience, having felt a similar pressure at work in my own case, and seen also, though fighting it every step of the way, how little choice I had in the matter.

An epic poem, ideally, needs to be backed by an elaborate and well-founded belief system. The author can, like Dante and Milton, begin with the ideas and beliefs current in his society, and elaborate on them imaginatively; or he can, like Blake, more or less construct his own system.

In *Sandover* the revelations of the Ouija board provided the belief system, and much of the poem was devoted to these revelations, all of which were received in prose. Not that Jimmy ever wholly abandoned the lyric: *Sandover* contains several fine shorter poems, as well as many striking lines and fragments. Part 1, *The Book of Ephraim*, is brilliant. The messages from beyond are treated lightly and kept to a minimum. Jimmy seems constantly aware of the difficulty of dealing with supernatural revelations in poetry:

To touch on these unspeakables you want
The spry nuances of a Bach courante

Or brook that running slips into a shawl
Of crystal noise—at last, the waterfall.

But as *Sandover* continues, Jimmy's own poetry occupies less and less space, and the pages are more and more crammed with the capital letters of messages from the Ouija board, few of them poetic and many beneath the level of good prose. As I read through the last two-thirds of the book I sometimes had the feeling that my friend's mind was intermittently being taken over by a stupid and possibly even evil alien intelligence.

Jimmy of course knew that the Ouija board transcripts were not great poetry or prose; that they were often clumsy, repetitive, or even unintelligible. Moreover, there was far too much material: many thousands of pages recorded over nearly thirty years. Only a very small proportion of this material would appear in the final poem, after a great deal of editing and revision, as David Jackson's brief but suggestive essay "Lending a Hand" points out:

Messages I'd remembered as nearly meaningless [were] now charged with meaning; . . .

As the poem progressed I was always astonished by my own fascination, as if I were listening to an orchestration of what had been a wobbly or inharmonic melody.

The title of the trilogy, *The Changing Light at Sandover*, can be read in various ways. On its first appearance, "Sandover" is the imaginary mansion of English poetry described by the spirit of Auden in *Mirabell*, Book 9:

. . . THE ROSEBRICK MANOR
ALL TOPIARY FORMS & METRICAL
MOAT ARIPPLE!

Later, Jimmy suggests that perhaps *"The name is a corruption of the French / Saintefleur"*—that is, "Holy Flower." But in English the word "Sandover" suggests that something—a building, a person, or a memory—has been or is being buried in sand. Or, as the poem hints later, it could describe the action of an hourglass, which stands for time.

"The Changing Light" suggests both that time is passing and that, as it does, things and people begin to look very different—just as they do in a less distressing way in Claude Monet's many views of the same haystack at different times of day. And, indeed, as the poem progresses, both humans and spirits change radically.

The titles of the individual sections of *Sandover* are

also ambiguous. Part 1 first appeared in a volume of poems called *Divine Comedies*—a clear reference to Dante—as *The Book of Ephraim*, suggesting a prophetic book of the Bible. Part 2, *Mirabell's Books of Number*, also recalls the Bible (the Book of Numbers). Part 3, *Scripts for the Pageant*, on the other hand, suggests that perhaps the whole enterprise is a dramatic production and/or a ritual—and also, possibly, that this show might eventually be staged. This of course was a hint that was taken up much later by Jimmy's friend Peter Hooten, with very mixed results.

6

Good News from the
Other World

✳

No matter what method is used to consult the supernatural, four main sorts of message are traditionally received. First, and most common, are reassuring communications from one's deceased friends and relatives. Those who have "passed over" are almost always well and happy; they still love you and are watching over you.

When I was researching my third novel, *Imaginary Friends*, I often heard such communications during visits to what I shall call the Sophis Spiritualist Conference. The general tone of their meetings was Christian, low-key, and amicable. After hymns and prayers, a visiting medium would give a short inspiring sermon; then he or she would go into a trance and bring the congregation messages from their lost loved ones.

These messages were usually brief, upbeat, and rather vague. I, for instance, heard that my grandmother—whom I had never met—sent her good wishes to me and my family, and that sometime in the next few months I would receive an unexpected visit from an old friend—a fairly safe guess, I thought at the time. The spirits often made predictions of this sort, almost always positive ones. They also gave useful advice: people were told to have faith and hope in the future, to eat less and exercise more, to give practical help and spiritual comfort to "someone less fortunate than you."

Often the recipient of the messages was self-selected. "There are many, many spirits around us tonight," a medium once announced, speaking in the deeper and more ringing tones of her spirit guide, a sixteenth-century New England settler called Patience. "One who is coming to me now has a name that begins with the letter A, and she wants to speak to her sister. Does anyone here recognize her?" Instantly, as might have been expected, two elderly members of the congregation raised their hands. Those who did not volunteer during the course of the meeting also received messages, so that by the end of the evening everyone had had a spirit communication.

*

For some reason, souls in the spirit world seldom manifest themselves independently. Whether they come through a human medium or via the Ouija board, they are usually introduced by a spirit guide, who acts as a kind of social director, sorting out the crowds of ghosts who want to communicate with the living. Spirit guides have often died young or been especially enlightened in life. In the nineteenth century many were deceased Native Americans, and this tradition continues: one medium whose séance I attended had two spirit guides, a giggly six-year-old named Betty and a dignified Iroquois called Chief Eagle.

Jimmy and David's spirit guide, Ephraim, presently put them in contact with several loved and lost friends, beginning with Hans Lodeizen (1924–50), a young Dutch poet whom Jimmy had known in Europe, and Maya Deren (1917–61), the American experimental filmmaker. Later, as more friends died, they also communicated through the Ouija board. Other ghosts who had been unknown to either Jimmy or David sometimes tried to muscle in:

Once stroked, once fed by us, stray souls maneuver
Round the teacup for a chance to glide
(As DJ yawns, quick!) to the warmth inside.

Occasionally the person who had passed on was someone with whom my friends' relationship had been difficult. As at the Sophis Spiritualist Conference, these ghostly reappearances could be very reassuring. Jimmy's father, the somewhat overpowering financial tycoon Charles E. Merrill, died in 1960, when Jimmy and David were in Japan. Jimmy, uneasy because he wasn't overcome with grief and also because he couldn't or wouldn't be able to get back to America in time for the funeral, was reassured by the spirit of "a young Zen priest centuries old," who explained that his coolness and detachment were in fact admirable. And when "CEM" himself finally got through on the supernatural telegraph, he announced that

He loved his wives, his other children, me;
Looks forward to his next life. Would not be
Weeping in *my* shoes.

David's conservative Republican parents, especially his father, had always disapproved of his homosexuality while alive. After death, however, they came round.

David's mother was affectionate and consoling, though (as in life) somewhat confused. And his father, though still crude and unenlightened at first, now accepted David and Jimmy's relationship ("YOU 2 ARE OK"), though he was of no practical use:

> Dad, just tell me where the bankbooks are?
> WHAT FOR   CANT TAKE IT WITH U (long pause)
>   NONE
> I GUESS THINGS GOT EXPENSIVE   TOO BAD SON

Soon, however, David's father began to see the light and apologize for his past behavior:

> DEAR SON FORGIVE ME   NEVER LET MONEY SOUR U
> I PITY THE OLD ME

Later on in the poem David's parents lose their individual voices and begin to send banal spiritualist messages: WE HAVE LIVED & LOVED / & FELT YR LOVE   LET US GO FORTH ANEW.

❋

Two dead friends presently became important communicants—and later major characters in the *Sandover* trilogy—the poet W. H. Auden (1907–73) and the Greek aristocrat Maria Mitsotáki (1907–74). Maria had been a close friend; Auden, though David and Jimmy had not known him well in this world, became equally close as a ghost. At first one of Jimmy and David's spirit guides had to be there to introduce them, but eventually both Maria and Auden were able to communicate without assistance. Or rather, to take a skeptical view, the imaginary Maria and the imaginary Auden had by then been so clearly reimagined that it was easy to produce their voices.

I had never met Maria, and had only heard Auden speak on public and semipublic (English Department reception) occasions, so I accepted their voices as more or less characteristic. But when the ghosts of people I had known well in life began to manifest themselves, they didn't seem real. At best they sounded mannered and repetitious, as if they were ill or somehow distracted. Of course, we all have slightly different voices for different friends, I thought. The ghosts were speaking to David and Jimmy, not to me; maybe that was why they seemed unfamiliar.

*

Another common role of the Ouija board is to bring its users messages from famous dead persons. Apparently, celebrities from everywhere in the world and over three thousand years of history are eager to communicate with contemporary housewives and small businessmen, secretaries and schoolteachers, teenagers and senior citizens. Egyptian pharaohs and Greek philosophers, European kings and queens, and world-renowned writers and artists and musicians crowd into small-town sitting rooms to discuss art, religion, philosophy, and current events.

In my friends' case the incongruity at first seemed less, since after all they had known celebrities; also, many of their early visitants were people whose years on the material plane had been relatively obscure. But in the end Jimmy and David, too—or their spirit guides—gradually succumbed to the fascination with fame so prevalent today. Literary figures they had known only slightly or not at all began to appear: Gertrude Stein, Wallace Stevens, W. B Yeats, T. S. Eliot, and even poets from past centuries like Andrew Marvell and Emily Dickinson. My friends also spoke familiarly with composers such as Hindemith, Wagner, and Richard Strauss.

So besieged by the spirits of celebrities were they eventually that on occasion they turned one away. There is a running joke in *Sandover* in which David and Jimmy decline to speak to the author of *Lolita*:

Good News from the Other World

. . . A MR NABOKOV LEFT HIS NAME
Please, not today.

One problem about communication with the famous
dead, especially if they are writers, is that it is difficult
to reproduce the individual voice of a genius even if
you are a genius yourself. Andrew Marvell's preference
for formalist verse is understandable, but he expresses it
in a style that seems more Jimmy's than his own:

. . . 'THE LINE, MY DEAR NEW FRIEND,
THE LINE! LET IT RUN TAUT & FLEXIBLE
BETWEEN THE TWO POLES OF RHYTHM & RHYME,
& WHAT YOU HANG ON IT MAY BE AS DULL
OR AS PROVOCATIVE AS LAUNDRY.'

Yeats's dialogue seems a clumsy parody, although Jimmy
once admits in the poem that he has been "up tinker-
ing since dawn" revising it. Auden comes through the
Ouija board believably in prose, but his poetry seems
mostly a pastiche. (Perhaps that is why his spirit comments at one point "SO MADDENING / NOT TO REVISE").
Only late in the final volume of the trilogy is there a
convincing example of his verse, which echoes the
songs from *The Rake's Progress*.

ONE SAILOR'S CLEAR

YOUNG TENOR FILLS THE HOUSE, HOMESICK,

HEARTSICK.

THE MAST NEEDS COMFORT. GALES

HAVE TATTERED THE MOONBELLIED SAILS.

MAY HIS GREEN SHORES O QUICKLY

SAFELY NOW FROM RAGING FOAM APPEAR.

The notion of a living writer communicating with his dead colleagues has a certain appropriateness, even charm. But real problems arise in part 3 of *Sandover*, where Buddha, Mohammed, and finally even Jesus appear.

※

The third characteristic type of message from the supernatural world is that the receivers of these communications are special people. They are greatly loved and admired by the spirits, and have often been chosen by them for a special purpose. Also, in the spirit world, they are eternally young and beautiful.

Like fond parents, the spirits in *Sandover* are sometimes more enthusiastic about Jimmy's work than he is himself. After he begins to write and publish sections of *The Book of Ephraim*, Ephraim himself declares that he

and many other spirits, including some who were difficult to please in life, like Alice B. Toklas and Marius
Bewley, "all burn / To read more of this poem."

Throughout *Sandover* Ephraim continually praises
and flatters David and Jimmy, declaring that they are
enlightened beings, superior to most humans and farther along on the Path. In a sense this information fol-
lows logically from what has gone before. If wise and
noble spirits and the famous dead have chosen to communicate with you, you are clearly exceptional.

In fact, praise of Jimmy and David in *Sandover* eventually becomes almost embarrassing, however much
one might admire them. The peacock and possible
fallen angel Mirabell, for instance, tells them that there
is a "RADIANCE AROUND U" and that

    . . . YR FIELD IS
    YES A KIND OF ANCHOR POINT OF HEAVEN. O
        SCRIBE, O HAND
    U HAVE PAID YR DUES AGAIN & AGAIN . . .
    . . . U
    WHO ARE OUR LOVED ONES

God Biology himself is looking after them:

. . . HIS WARNING TO EVEN HIS WHITE
ANGELS IS: BEHOLD THESE ARE MY OWN
   DARLINGS   THEIR MISTAKES
ARE NOT SUCH IN MY EYES
THEY DO NOT FAIL ME   TO BUILD THEIR
PARADISE IS MY WORK   DO NOT INTERFERE WITH
   THEIR LIVES.

Few short-term users of the Ouija board, or clients of professional mediums, receive this kind of over-the-top praise. At the Sophis Spiritualist Conference deceased friends and relatives often spoke warmly of the living, and so, occasionally, did the medium's spirit guides: "Betty says you are a very sweet lady, and there is a pink light around you." But most of the other members of the audience soon turned out to be sweet ladies or nice men, too, and they were sometimes quietly warned against spiritual pride and/or earthly vanity.

*

When users of the Ouija board—or any similar device—persist in their explorations, they often begin to receive information about the structure of the invisible world. Since they have been chosen by supernatural entities, it seems logical that knowledge of supernatural geography, history, and administration should be revealed to them. Sometimes communicants are instructed that it is their duty to share this information with other, less-enlightened souls: that they must form a church or a movement. Other seekers are told that they must keep this secret knowledge to themselves, or share it only partially. Professional spirit mediums, for instance, are usually vague about conditions on the other side of the veil. At the Sophis Spiritualist Conference, the congregation was merely told that Heaven was a happy and beautiful place, full of light and music. More than that the mediums either did not know, or would not say. But when we had Passed Over, they assured us, all would be clear.

Much of *The Changing Light at Sandover* consists of the secret doctrine that was gradually revealed to David and Jimmy. As it unfolds, the system becomes more and more complex, fantastic and all-encompassing. It also, at least to me, becomes more deeply disturbing— whether I think of it as literally true or as metaphor, as deliberately produced or as an unconscious outpouring.

*

In part 1 of *Sandover*, *The Book of Ephraim*, news of the spirit world is communicated informally and anecdotally, and is of a sort familiar to most students of comparative religion or New Age publications. Jimmy and

David learn that everyone now alive is the "REPRESEN-TATIVE OF A PATRON," a kind of secular guardian angel, once human, who watches over us but usually can't interfere. On earth we live many different lives, and if we do well in them we advance gradually, becoming more and more enlightened. Eventually we cease to be reborn; then we remain in the spirit world, becoming patrons of new, as yet not fully enlightened, souls.

Early on in *Sandover*, Ephraim arranges for the soul currently in his care—"a feeble nature / All but bestial, given to violent / Short lives"—to be reborn as the son of Jimmy's pregnant niece—no favor to her, one might think. But when, nearly twenty years later, Jimmy meets the grown-up baby in Venice, he is not only nonviolent and presentable but has become an artist. And, like Jimmy, he has an artist's detachment:

He rather looks down on the scene, I sense,
Or through it—not for nothing are we kin

Parts 2 and 3 of *Sandover* continue to explain the invisible world, but now in a much more lengthy, organized, and—some have felt—tedious way. Instead of entertaining tales of reincarnation, we are given an elaborate, ever-expanding mystical system, which eventually includes some rather surprising information about history, religion, literature, art, and science.

The bulk of *Mirabell* and *Scripts for the Pageant* consists of lessons held in an invisible but vividly imagined schoolroom for four students: my two friends and, on the other side of the veil, the spirits of W. H. Auden and Maria Mitsotáki. Perhaps it was natural for the transmission of mystical wisdom to take academic form, since much of Jimmy's and David's early lives had been spent in school, either as students or teachers. Jimmy, David, Auden, and Maria all turn out to be excellent students, whom their invisible instructors keep encouraging with praise and high grades ("INDEED   A PLUS").

From one part to the next the spirit tutors become more and more grand and authoritative, just as in the terrestrial system simple grade-school teachers are replaced by more distant and demanding high-school teachers and finally by college professors. In part 1 their teacher is Ephraim, a former human being. Their next is a fallen angel known variously and ambiguously as "741," "Bezelbob," and "Mirabell," who takes the form first of a bat and then of a peacock. In part 3 of the trilogy, the four students are instructed by the four archangels, and finally by God himself.

The invisible world, according to *Sandover*, is complex and hierarchical. At the top of the pyramid is God (also known as God Biology or God B) and just below him Nature, known also as Psyche and Chaos, and described as "AT ONCE FECUND & LAZY. . . . A FAVORITE SLAVE." Jimmy and David are informed that "THE MALE REIGNS IN NUMBER, THE FEMALE IN NATURE"; scientific order is superior and male, natural disorder is inferior and female.

Next in rank below God B and Nature come the four archangels: Michael, Emmanuel, Raphael, and Gabriel, each associated with one of the four elements; Gabriel, for instance, is the Angel of Fire and Death. They are followed by the Nine Muses and the minor angels, one of whom is Mirabell.

Just below this is a group of noble, formerly human souls known as "THE DEATHLESS 5." In their original incarnations they were the pharaoh Akhnaton, Homer, Montezuma, Nefertiti, and Plato—but they have taken on many other human lives since then. They are followed by four religious leaders: Gautama, Jesus, Mercury, and Mohammed. Below this is a hodgepodge collection of enlightened souls that contains many dead friends and acquaintances of Jimmy and David, and others unknown to them in life, including Ephraim, Maria Callas, and Pythagoras. A white unicorn called Unice, who seems to be a kind of Pegasus figure, brings up the rear.

All humans who have ever lived may be classified numerically in various ways. The most admirable have a "talent rating"; the lower and nearer the number is to 5 (the number of the Deathless), the better: Jimmy and David "ARE BOTH PARTIAL 5s." "PEOPLE OF PHYSICAL PROWESS & LEGENDARY HEROES" are Sixes, at the next lower level—a piece of information sure to please any intellectual but nonathletic reader.

The main work of Heaven, according to the lessons of *Sandover,* is to create improved human souls. These souls are manufactured somewhere in outer space in what is known as the "Research Lab," using bits of former souls, chemicals like salt and radium, and complicated mathematical formulae.

Most souls, however, are "NOT USABLE" in the Research Lab because they have too much animal density. Due to overpopulation, there isn't enough human soul material to go around, and many people living today have souls largely composed of the animal densities of dog and rat. There are billions of these second-rate,

> . . . run-of-the-mill souls who
> Life by life, under domed thicknesses,
> Plod the slow road of Earth—

A few of these second-rate souls have been very successful on Earth, unfortunately, and much world power is now in the hands of leaders who are essentially dogs and rats.

After death, all imperfect souls are discarded by the Research Lab in a manner that Mirabell compares to what happens in the garbage disposal in Jimmy's kitchen:

> I WATCH U COOK   U HAVE A MACHINE THAT EATS
>   USELESS THINGS
> THIS IS THE (M) FATE OF USELESS LIVES

The spirits devote themselves to an elite of at most two million souls, among whom are their present students.

> . . . WE CLONE THE HAPPY FEW   THE MASSES
>   WE NEED
> NEVER CONSIDER   THEY REMAIN IN AN ANIMAL
>   STATE

Elite souls are composed of different metals: Auden, for instance, is platinum, Jimmy silver, David (to his dismay) merely "A NICE MIX OF SILVER & TIN." Moreover, the soul material from someone now discarnate may be added to an existing human soul, increasing its worth.

A related and recurrent theme of *Sandover* is over-population. There are too many people on the planet, and something must be done about this:

> . . . TOO MANY
> FRACTIONAL HUMANS ON EARTH   THE NEXT RACE
>   WILL BE OF GODS

The spirits are continually working to "THIN POPU-LATION & KEEP IT PREDOMINANTLY RURAL," using both natural and manmade disasters for this purpose. As Mirabell disturbingly puts it:

> . . . WE ONLY WISH TO PURIFY
> CERTAIN RANCID ELEMENTS FROM THIS ELITE
>   BUTTER WORLD.
> THE HITLERS THE PERONS & FRANCOS   THE
>   STALINS . . .
> . . . ARE NEEDED

Throughout *Sandover* the spirits often take this chilly, antidemocratic tone. Often it disturbs both David and Auden. Later David remarked in his interview with Sandy McClatchy that "As Wystan, I think, points out, it's awful to be a liberal and hear all this elitist shit." Nevertheless both Auden and David, as well as Jimmy, apparently come to accept it. The aristocratic Maria never appears to question the doctrine.

Within the poem David and Jimmy also seem remarkably comfortable with the authoritarian demands of the spirits—perhaps understandable if one assumes that these demands are only the expression of their own subconscious wishes. But I was disturbed to discover that they had decided not to investigate the identity of the spirits who made these demands:

> Who They were it seemed wiser not to know
> yet. . . .
> Here in Stonington at last, it matters
> Less that we understand them than obey.

As *Sandover* progresses, the information Jimmy and David receive becomes more complex, and begins to reflect Jimmy's Ouija-inspired reading of books on biology and evolution and genetics. The spirits manage to "explain" many of the current scientific and pseudo-scientific puzzles: black holes, nuclear energy, flying saucers, Atlantis, Stonehenge, the Bermuda Triangle, etc.

Perhaps it was easier for Jimmy to accept a semi-mystical, semiscientific spirit world because he had no strong preexisting knowledge or convictions that might have conflicted with it. The Ouija board gave him a belief system, and he didn't question it as a writer with a scientific background, or strong religious or political commitments, might have done. As he wrote in *Ephraim:*

> . . . In neither
> The world's poem nor the poem's world have I
> Learned to think for myself, much.

Any imaginary world, of course, tends to bear traces of the world its inventors already know, and to incorporate their life experiences, memories, and dreams, their ideas about science, morality, and the arts. The resulting construct will inevitably reflect its creators' knowledge, opinions, and tastes, both conscious and unconscious. It was so with the mysterious universe described in *Sandover.*

For example, both David and Jimmy were brought up as Protestants: it is thus unsurprising, if a little disappointing, to learn that "THE XTIAN MYTHS U KNOW COME CLOSEST TO THESE EARTHY TRUTHS," while "THE KORAN ALAS IS A WORK / PATCHD TOGETHER BY A NOMAD RACE."

Characteristically, it also turns out that the two "essential" arts are poetry and music; drama, fiction, and architecture are slightly inferior. As for the graphic arts, even "the great paintings" are said to "CONTAIN NO LIGHT." They are:

ALL BLACK   UNLIT   AT BEST SPIRITUAL
    EXERCISES . . .
ONLY MUSIC & WORDS IMPLICATE THAT LIGHT
    WHICH BOTH SHEDS
& ATTRACTS

Considering that David was not only a novelist but a painter, reading this for the first time made me uneasy. Did it express Jimmy's mild scorn of art and fiction, or David's own self-doubt and even self-hatred?

According to *Sandover*, poets (as others have said) must become our lawmakers and our priests, and thus "DEVELOP THE WAY TO P A R A D I S E":

. . . The innate
Role of the Scribe must now be to supplant
Religion.

But even among poets there is hierarchy in the spirit world. Some are doing well; others, like Edna Millay, remain stuck at a very low level. Byron suffers from "ESSENTIAL HOKUM & GALLANTRY," Wallace Stevens is a

"DRY SCRIBE," Goethe and Rilke are dull, and Whitman has become "HALF WITLESS" because so much of his soul material has been "MINED" to create other poets. (Translation, perhaps: he has too many imitators.)

In *Mirabell* and *Scripts* there are communications from many poets and musicians—but no writers of prose are contacted. (It is possible that my pointing this out to Jimmy, or the similar comments of other readers, were responsible for the sudden appearance of Jane Austen and Dickens in the brief *Coda*, published for the first time at the end of *Sandover*.

Another prominent aspect of the *Sandover* system is that the population of Heaven is largely male. Even Maria, Jimmy and David's beloved Greek friend, turns out to be a male spirit who merely disguised herself as a fag hag in her latest earthly life. She/he explains that she played her human role "IN DRAG, / I LOVE IT . . . THESE ESCAPES INTO A FEMALE LIFE ARE VAST / REFRESHMENTS." During this life, she/he confides, David and Jimmy and another gay friend were "THE RICH SOIL OF / MY LAST BLOOMING."

Along with this emphasis on the male sex, there is the repeated idea that homosexuality is a superior condition. All four students in *Sandover*, after all, turn out to be essentially male and gay. Homosexuality, the spirits teach them,

IS A NEW DEVELOPMENT OF THE PAST 4000 YEARS
ENCOURAGING SUCH MIND VALUES AS PRODUCE
   THE BLOSSOMS
OF POETRY & MUSIC, THOSE 2 PRINCIPAL LIGHTS OF
GOD BIOLOGY.

David, Jimmy, Auden, and Maria have been selected both because of their childlessness, and also because "THE LOVE ⁄ U EXPERIENCE IS NOT THE STRAIGHT-FORWARD FRONTAL LOVE."

These personal biases are understandable and forgivable. But a disturbing note is struck in part 2 when Mirabell informs Jimmy and David that souls have different "densities," which are carefully calibrated by the spirits, and that the "Density in man par excellence" is "Jew," which must be used sparingly in creating a soul:

Human uranium. . . .
. . . Infinite care goes
Into the prescription and the dose.

The Jewish race was established in the Near East when

A MIGRANT STRAIN OF FRESHEST JEWSTOCK TRAILD
   ACROSS CHINA
TO A RESOURCEFUL INSULARITY . . .
BUT THEY TOO OVERPRODUCE & ARE NO LONGER
   OUR HOPE

The "COMPETITIVE ELEMENT," Mirabell adds later, "IS AN ORIGINAL JEW DENSITY." Since their first spirit guide, Ephraim, and many of David and Jimmy's closest friends were Jewish, and I had always thought of them as wholly without prejudice, I was surprised and depressed to come upon these passages, which I suppose must have bubbled up from someone's subconscious in an unguarded moment.

7

─────

How and Why

✳

WHEN COHERENT MESSAGES ARE RECEIVED from a
Ouija board, there are three possible explanations. First,
it may be that deceased humans and/or supernatural
beings are communicating with us, or trying to.

Second, it may be that one or both of the sitters, out
of boredom and impatience, or a sudden mischievous
impulse, has been cheating: moving the pointer deliberately. It is possible to do this without detection: as an
adolescent, I once did it myself. Watching David and
Jimmy at the board, I noticed that David's right hand
was on the teacup; he was referred to by the spirits

as HAND. Jimmy's left hand was on the cup, and he recorded its messages with his right; he was referred to as SCRIBE. My first guess was that while Jimmy was busy writing the messages down, David was gently but firmly pushing the teacup. Later this seemed to me a simplification, though I still think that he may have done so sometimes. In the final years, for instance, when he was often openly impatient with the Ouija board sessions, it is possible that he at least half-consciously produced the occasionally contradictory, shocking, or even silly messages that were sometimes received.

Third, the pointer may be pushed by the sitters without their conscious volition. In this case there are again two possibilities. First, one of the sitters may be moving it, allowing messages to emerge from his subconscious in a dreamlike manner. (The sitters may, of course, take turns doing this.) Second, the two of them may collaborate unconsciously, pooling their powers. This could explain why, as Jimmy put it early in *Ephraim,* "even the most fragmentary message" seemed "Twice as entertaining, twice as wise / As either of its mediums."

According to writers on the Ouija board, one of the sitters always turns out to be the essential conduit to the spirit world. He or she may not be able to receive messages alone, but nobody can receive messages from these particular spirits unless he or she is present. In my friends' case the essential sitter was clearly David. He was more skeptical about the external reality of the spirits, but he was also more afraid of them. And he was also more attuned to their existence. Jimmy used to maintain, only partly in jest, that David had ESP, though David was skeptical about this too. When Sandy McClatchy asked how early in David's life he was aware of that gift, he replied:

> I don't think I ever was. There was this legend in my family that I was born with a caul. . . . And I had a German nurse, Frau Schnitzel, who claimed that babies with cauls had second sight.

Sometimes his nurse seemed to have been right. For example, David had the ability, not uncommon, of often knowing who was calling when the phone rang. "That's Eleanor," he would say, and he would be correct.

Also, unlike Jimmy, David might be said to have had what used to be called a split personality—or, at least, one capable of sudden changes of manner and mood. He was also far more suggestible psychologically; he was, for instance, an excellent hypnotic subject. Jimmy was able to put him into a trance quite easily, and take him back into his past, where he would relive early memories. Once I heard him, very vividly, recall his fifth birthday.

Today memories recovered under hypnosis are suspected of being, most of the time, pure fantasy. We didn't know this then, and I was eager to relive my own fifth birthday. So one evening in Stonington Jimmy tried to hypnotize me, and I tried hard to go under— but without success. I have never been susceptible to hypnosis, nor, to his expressed regret, was Jimmy; David could not hypnotize him and neither could anyone else.

Under hypnosis David had some peculiar experiences. Early on, in Amherst, as he told Sandy Mc-Clatchy, he had a vision of their spirit guide, Ephraim.

It was winter, we were often snowed in, and six or seven miles from town . . . the two of us alone with time on our hands, or nights alone, in a remote place.

David saw Ephraim reflected in a window, as a beautiful young man with golden eyes and hair. Later, Jimmy incorporated David's description of him into *Sandover*. He had:

the limbs & torso muscled by long folds of
an unemasculated Blake nude. Who then
actually was in the room, at arm's length, . . .
. . . His smile was that of an old friend, so
casual. . . .
. . . He somehow was
using me, my senses, to touch JM

Some years later, on a foggy night in Stonington, David saw a white face pressed flat against the black glass of the window of the room where he and Jimmy were consulting the spirits—a window three stories up, looking out only on the night air. The apparition's eyes were shut, its mouth open in a scream, and David knew it was a demon, trying to get in. Jimmy could see neither Ephraim nor the Stonington demon. But in *Sandover* he records how on another occasion, in Athens, the spirits instructed David: "PLACE / YR FREE HAND PALMDOWN YES ON THE BOARDS EDGE." He obeyed, and both he and Jimmy saw David's hand become "creased, red, sore / As if it had been trod on for attention." David could not move his hand; in spite of his fear and growing impatience with the spirits, he was literally and metaphorically pinned to the board.

How and Why

＊

There are, in most people's minds, dark corners and unfriendly forces. And these internal enemies in some cases can be more dangerous than external ones. If a message floats up out of your subconscious, even if it is violent or mad, it often has a kind of aura of rightness and power. Like some dreams, it may seem truer and stronger than reality.

Still, when you are fully awake, or the game is put away, the rational mind usually takes over. Amused, excited, intrigued as they were, did either Jimmy or David ever wholly believe in the messages they received during their séances? I think the answer is, Not wholly, not always.

In *Sandover* several passages suggest that David and Jimmy knew quite well that the spirit world they had called up was an imaginative construct. Early on, Jimmy calls the messages "A strangeness that was us, and was not." Later the spirits themselves put the same observation more subtly, saying, "WE ARE U YOU ARE WE EACH OTHERS DREAM." And even deep into the fantasy of the invisible schoolroom where two of the students are ghosts, Jimmy breaks into the lesson to remind their teacher Mirabell that:

. . . you are not
A person, not a peacock, not a bat;
A devil least of all—an impulse only
Here at the crossroads of our four affections.

They knew, too, that the ghosts of their dead friends were makeshift constructs. Once, when Jimmy addresses Maria, he reminds her in a line that is almost Shakespearean that "You see with our minds' eye, with nothing else."

※

And yet in spite of this knowledge, Jimmy and David went on, month after month, year after year, communicating with invisible, presumably self-created entities. Now and then one of my friends, most often David, questions what they are doing:

The blue room after dinner. DJ (depressed):
Each day it grows more fascinating, more . . .
I don't know. Isn't it like a door
Shutting us off from living? I've no zest
For anything else, can't even watch TV.
This town's full of good friends we hardly see.

Occasionally both David and Jimmy, especially the former, told me they were tired of the Ouija board.

Sometimes they left it alone for weeks or months, once for almost four years; but they always returned, at times under what seemed to them like supernatural pressure. And in spite of his doubts and fears, David continued to give hours and days of his life, and much of his energy, to the spirits, and to justify doing so. As late as 1978 he would tell Sandy McClatchy that "the experience of the ouija board was just divine, in every sense," and express regret as well as relief when it was over and the poem finished.

*

When two sophisticated, extremely intelligent people devote over twenty-five years to recording messages from imaginary beings, you have to ask, What was in it for them? There are, I think, several answers to this question, some of which Jimmy himself listed in *Sandover*:

Ephraim's revelations—we had them
For comfort, thrills and chills, "material."

That is, reassurance, excitement, and literary inspiration.

Metaphorically speaking, all writing is the transcription of messages from your unconscious—you write down words that were not in your conscious mind a few minutes ago. But almost from the first the communications from the Ouija board were important source material for Jimmy. From the spirit messages, plus descriptions of and meditations on their role in his and David's lives, he eventually created many pages of poetry.

He did not, however, simply write to the dictation of the spirits: *Sandover* involved a great deal of editing. There were thousands of pages of transcripts, and as David revealed in his brief but fascinating essay, "Lending a Hand," Jimmy condensed and rewrote extensively.

The result of all this work was one brilliant long poem, *Ephraim*, of which the spirits' words occupy only a small part, and three less impressive sequels, *Mirabell* and *Scripts for the Pageant* and a short *Coda: The Higher Keys*. *Ephraim* is a tour de force, an original and amazing collection of twenty-six poems in an astounding variety of forms, some of them among the best Jimmy ever wrote. Composing it was both absorbing and estranging. In January 1976 Jimmy wrote me from Athens:

Ephraim should be out in a month or so. I had to read proof twice and even phone in final corrections . . . from here. I feel all empty, blinking about at the real world—what there is of it. (January 22, 1976)

How and Why

After *Ephraim* Jimmy was determined to move on:

> ... No more spirits, please.
> No statelier mansions. No wanting to be Pope.
> Ephraim's book is written now, is shut.

But someone or something wanted him to continue. In 1975 the final illness of David's parents, and the death of two friends, brought them back to the Ouija board ("As things were, / Where else to look for sense, comfort and wit?"). And very soon

> Whoever the Powers are we've been avoiding
> Take possession, speed us far downstream
> Through gorges echoing at the pitch of dream.

Before long these Powers begin demanding that Jimmy write about them again:

> ... WE WANT   WE MUST HAVE
> POEMS OF SCIENCE

Obediently, Jimmy returned to Stonington alone and started to read biology, physics, and chemistry texts; and when David joined him the following summer, they began to consult the Ouija board again seriously.

Writing Poems of Science might be difficult, but there were consolations: halfway through *Mirabell* Jimmy confesses

> . . . I once was piercingly
> Aware of (metaphor) black holes in me:
> Waste, self-hatred, boredom. One by one,
> These weeks here at the Board, they've been erased.

When Jimmy began *Ephraim* a long time had passed since the events it describes, and he had had time to meditate on the experience. With *Mirabell* and *Scripts*, however, he was trying to transform the Ouija board messages into poetry almost immediately, and the results were uneven.

Though the spirits continually encourage him, and even demand that he continue, now and then he protests. Towards the end of *Mirabell*, when Auden declares:

ON WITH THE WORK! THRILLING FOR U JM

Jimmy's response is:

> And maddening—it's all by someone else!
> In your voice, Wystan, or in Mirabell's.

Only just now, copying these lines, did I notice that Auden does not suggest that the "work" is thrilling for DJ. If this was a disguised message from David to Jimmy, he didn't seem to receive it. Instead he focused on his own creative difficulties:

I want it mine, but cannot spare those twenty
Years in a cool dark place that *Ephraim* took . . .
. . . I'd set
My whole heart, after *Ephraim*, on returning
To private life, to my own words. Instead,
Here I go again, a vehicle
In this cosmic carpool.

Overhearing Jimmy's complaint, Auden's spirit chides him in what sounds rather like the voice of a poststructuralist critic:

YR SCRUPLES DEAR BOY ARE INCONSEQUENT
IF I MAY SAY SO   CAN U STILL BE BENT, . . .
ON DOING YR OWN THING: EACH TEENY BIT
(PARDON MME) MADE PERSONAL AS SHIT? . . .
. . . THINK WHAT A MINOR
PART THE SELF PLAYS IN A WORK OF ART

(Passages like this, incidentally, can't help but remind a reader that the Ouija-board Auden is an artificial construct.)

As it turned out, Jimmy would not have twenty years to spare; but it might have been better if he had allowed this new material to sit for a while. In *Sandover* he created a remarkable but uneven work, and at a cost.

❋

Another explanation of Jimmy and David's involvement with the Ouija board might focus on their personal situation. When they began to record the spirit messages in 1955 they were at a kind of crossroads in their life together. Three years earlier they had met and fallen in love, and for a while they were absorbed in this love. But even the most intense affair eventually needs a context: a plot, a setting, and important minor characters.

Jimmy and David had no permanent jobs and few family responsibilities. They were both independently rich: they could live anywhere and buy anything they wanted. Back in 1955 neither of their careers had really taken off. Though Jimmy's verse and his two short plays had been well reviewed, he was still almost unknown. He was nearly thirty; David was thirty-three. If they had been straight, they would have been at the peak of their attractiveness; but in the homosexual world, with its passion for extreme youth, they were no longer as romantically desirable as before. Were they, perhaps, irrelevant? And what were they to do with the rest of their lives?

What they did first was to spend much of the next year traveling around the world. It was a largely successful trip and inspired some fine poems. By the fall of 1957, though, they were back in Stonington, where the apartment seemed cramped and local off-season society boring. They weren't getting on as well as before, either:

> . . . Tediums
> Ignited into quarrels, each "a scene
> From real life," . . .
> David and I lived on, limbs thickening
> For better and worse in one another's shade.

But when they turned to the Ouija board Ephraim had a solution to their problems. They were not irrelevant or useless, he told them: they were superior, enlightened beings. Moreover, they were at the center of an invisible web of connections to lost friends and former selves past and present. And in the spirit world, they were later informed, they were eternally young and beautiful. Ephraim not only admired them but found them madly attractive: on one exceptionally spooky occasion, according to the poem, he appears to have taken control of David's body in order to possess Jimmy.

Ephraim also had an answer to their other question: What should they do now? His suggestion was that their lives should become more worldly and erotically various. Like him, they should take

FROM SENSUAL PLEASURE ONLY WHAT WILL NOT
DURING IT BE EVEN PARTLY SPOILED
BY FEAR OF LOSING TOO MUCH

In other words, Ephraim encouraged them to love promiscuously and superficially; to engage in the kind of sensual, disconnected erotic life they were soon to lead in Greece—that, in a sense, at Ephraim's suggestion, they went to Greece to lead. It was the obvious choice among the countries they'd visited on their travels; and after all Ephraim himself had been a Greek. In Athens they would abandon monogamy and yet remain loving friends, deeply loyal to each other. As Jimmy admitted later to David Kalstone, he began going to Greece "very much in the spirit of one who embarks upon a double life."

For the next twenty years, this plan worked fairly well. In Greece, they explained to me, the tradition of

Platonic love (in its original sense) was still alive. It was quite normal for young men in their teens to have an older male lover. The arrangement made sense, since most young Greek women were not available: they were still supposed to remain virgins until marriage, or at least until formally engaged, and before this they were closely chaperoned. Many young men were too poor (or too proud) to buy love, and though essentially straight, they were willing, even eager, to form a relationship with a "patron." Such a connection did not define a young man as homosexual, as long as it ended at twenty or so, and was followed by marriage and children. The patron was often accepted by both friends and family, especially if he were well-off and could give handsome presents. (Indeed, when another of Jimmy's young lovers got married, Jimmy paid for the wedding; later he helped the family emigrate, and dedicated a poem to their daughter.)

In the summer Athens was hot and crowded with tourists. Then Jimmy and David returned to Stonington, where the town was full of summer residents and amusing parties. Occasionally they would consult the Ouija board, but often they set it aside for months.

By 1965, however, the situation had changed. The main change was that Jimmy had become a successful writer, and David had not. Jimmy had now published three volumes of poetry, two novels, and two plays. David had nothing to show for ten years of work but a few stories and reviews, and four or five unpublished novels dying in a bottom drawer. Now he essentially gave up writing. For a while he occupied himself by painting small watercolors and pastels, mostly of buildings and interiors—and in 1978, in Athens, a mural of a classical Greek landscape that Jimmy was to describe later as an "ideal world."

> Four cream plaster columns catch the light;
> A path through olives; there, beyond the grove,
> A little beached skiff, an Arcadian cove.

All these works of art, though Jimmy admired them volubly, were at best decorative and pleasant; they expressed none of David's intelligence, energy, and originality.

David and Jimmy's renewed commitment to the Ouija board was a sort of answer, though a strange one, to this problem. From 1965 on, and especially between 1976 and 1982, David was profoundly involved in Jimmy's writing. And what he wrote got published: he was in an essential sense the co-author of *Sandover*, so much of which flowed through his hand, and none of which could have been written without him. One sign of this was that the messages from the spirits, like David's own writing, were in prose rather than poetry. If you believe, as I do, that his subconscious mainly guided the cup, more than half of the text of *Mirabell*, *Scripts*, and *Coda* was originally composed by him, and only later reshaped by Jimmy.

At one point the poem clearly suggests that this was so. When David learns from the spirits that the element that "defines" Jimmy is silver, while he is only "A NICE MIX OF SILVER & TIN," he cries:

. . . You see? There's no hope. I can't win.

The spirits reply:

THIS   THIS YR HOPE   CAN U NOT FEEL YRSELF
    SHAPING EVEN
NOW THIS PHRASE?

Uneasy, David asks, "Should I go back to writing novels?" but the spirits' answer, though politely phrased, seems to be No.

It is possible to see David's involvement in *Sandover* as an effort on Jimmy's part to prevent him from wasting his creative gift, to make him also a famous writer. If so, he failed; in spite of Jimmy's repeated emphasis on their partnership, almost everyone who has written on *Sandover* assumes that it was a one-man job, and David gets little credit for what the spirits say.

It is also possible to see the Ouija-board years as a last-ditch effort on the part of one or both of my friends to save the marriage. Night after night, as long as the collaboration continued, David and Jimmy were bound together in an intellectual and emotional partnership that necessarily excluded everyone else, including anyone either of them might be erotically involved with. Their union was approved by, even demanded by, powerful spirits—and also by the ghosts of their chosen parental figures, W. H. Auden and Maria Mitsotáki.

*

These were the advantages of their long, strange collaboration. But there are dangers in any connection with an unreal world, especially one that is shared to the point of *folie à deux*. Compared to the glamorous companionship and unconditional love and flattery offered by Auden and Maria, by divine beings, gods and ghosts, archangels and muses and supernatural peacocks, real life might seem drab, faded, even unreal. Jimmy knew this, of course. As he says in *Mirabell:*

—This outside world, our fictive darkness more
And more belittles to a safety door
Left open onto light. Too small, too far
To help. The blind bright spot of where we are.

The spot of where they are is bright, but it is also
blind. Jimmy recorded their doubts and fears, but he
and David did not put the Ouija board away; its rewards
were too great. As the poem continues, there are moments in which one or the other draws back. But
not usually at the same time, or for the same reasons. As
the spirits put it, Jimmy's and David's problems are
different:

. . . DOUBT IS YR HELL JM AS YOURS
DJ IS FEAR.

At one point in *Mirabell* Jimmy becomes restless, speaking of "our instructor's . . . encroaching obsolescence"
and comparing him to a TV set that can't be turned off.
David is more apt to wonder if the spirits are evil. Mid-
way through *Mirabell* he also asks if they will ever be
able to return to the world and live fully in it:

. . . Will that door readmit
Us to the world? Will we still care for it?

Jimmy, already deeply, perhaps dangerously, involved, suggests that like the heroes in Tolkien's *Lord of the Rings* they will

> . . . come through
> —It's what, in any Quest, the heroes do—
> But at the cost of being set apart,
> Emptied, diminished. Tolkien knew this. Art—
> The tale that all but shapes itself—survives
> By feeding on its personages' lives. . . .
> Our lives led *to* this. It's the price we pay.

In the end, both of them paid this price—but David paid it more heavily.

8

Doubts

✳

MOST PEOPLE who occasionally consult the supernatural, in whatever manner, waver in the intensity of their belief. In the first section of *Sandover* Jimmy and David's attitude towards the spirits fluctuates. Sometimes they seem true believers; at others they are skeptical or even frightened. At their first meeting with Ephraim, when they ask him if he is a devil, his ambiguous reply is "MY POOR INNOCENTS." A few lines later he demands their souls:

> Five whole minutes we were frightened stiff
> —But after all, we weren't *that* innocent.

The Rover Boys at thirty, still red-blooded
Enough not to pass up an armchair revel
And pure enough at heart to beat the devil

Afterwards Ephraim declares that he was just trying to scare them. The David and Jimmy who appear in the poem seem to forgive and then forget this episode—but I didn't. For me the answer to their question was Yes: metaphorically speaking, Ephraim was a devil, though perhaps a minor one.

A little later, a break in transmission occurs. Ephraim tells David and Jimmy that they have "MEDDLED," and then falls silent. Disturbed, Jimmy consults Tom, his "ex-shrink." The psychiatrist suggests that they have fallen into what he calls "folie à deux" and are practicing "psycho-roulette." That same evening Ephraim reappears and casts doubt on the doctor's insight, remarking that "FREUD . . . DESPAIRS / OF HIS DISCIPLES." Jimmy and David, happy to be reunited with their invisible friend and admirer, decide to dismiss the psychiatrist's warning and carry on. After all, it didn't matter where Ephraim came from:

. . . *He* was the revelation
(Or if we had created him, then we were).

As time passed, there were other uneasy moments. At the end of *Ephraim* Jimmy tells how one winter night, when they were out to dinner, their house in Stonington was broken into. Nothing of value was taken, but when he was cleaning up afterwards he found a displaced carton full of Ouija-board transcripts ("old love-letters from the other world"). He and David considered burning the papers, but desisted at the last moment. Speaking of the theft—and also, perhaps, of the spirits—Jimmy remarks:

> The threat remains, though, of there still being
> A presence in our midst, unknown, unseen,
> Unscrupulous to take what he can get.

In the second part of the trilogy, *Mirabell*, Jimmy describes how he and David returned to the Ouija board after over a year. He admits that they had given it up

> Half out of fears that now seemed idle, half
> Frankly out of having had our fill
> Of funeral cakes.

At first the reunion with the spirits is joyful, but soon there are ominous signs. In Athens they hear the doorbell ring but find only a black dog, "leg lifted at our iron gate / Marking his territory." Later, back in Stonington, sinister entities begin to appear—including one who announces himself as "BEZELBOB." These spirits deny that they are devils, but admit that

YOU WOULD NOT KNOW US AS MEN   WE HAVE
ONLY A DARK SHAPE

David and Jimmy's Greek friend Maria, now also in the spirit world, describes these beings as "QUITE LIKE BATS / HUGE SQUEAKING ONES WITH LITTLE HOT RED EYES." David, alarmed, wants to break off communication, but Jimmy insists on continuing. After all, he points out, "all this Flame and Fall / Has to be largely metaphorical." Possibly so, but as a Catholic friend warns in the poem, they were "playing with fire."

As time passes, the dark spirits make apparently plausible excuses for themselves ("THERE IS AN EVIL WE RELEASD WE DID NOT CREATE IT") and gradually metamorphose into more agreeable forms. David and Jimmy's principal instructor, Mirabell, turns from bat into peacock and begins to give out pages and pages of complex and often vague information about the spiritual, astronomical, historical, and biological world.

Doubts

At first Jimmy questions the blurry New Age content of these messages:

> . . . all this
> Warmed-up Milton, Dante, Genesis?
> This great tradition that has come to grief
> In volumes by Blavatsky and Gurdjieff? . . .
> Nobody can transfigure junk like that
> Without first turning down the rheostat
> To Allegory, in whose gloom the whole
> Horror of Popthink fastens on the soul

At times the highfalutin philosophical content of the lessons also troubled him. At a symposium in Washington, D.C., in 1982, he remarked:

> I've noticed in my own work, to my horror, writing this trilogy, that suddenly everything was getting much bigger than I thought a life should be. I kept clinging to the idea of Elizabeth [Bishop] with her sanity and levelheadedness.

But in spite of his doubts he goes on recording the ever-lengthening messages. As *Sandover* continues, the capital letters of the transcripts expand, covering more and more space, while his own lower-case comments shrink: telegraphic prose crowds out poetry. Several of David's and Jimmy's friends seem to have had negative reactions to these instructional spirit messages, and Jimmy sometimes includes these reactions in *Sandover*. For instance, Robert Morse, a Stonington neighbor who was a classical pianist and a shrewd observer of local life, remarks after reading some of the transcripts of spirit communications:

> . . . Me giddy fwom
> Uppercut of too much upper case. . . .
>
> In this guidebook of yours, how do you tell
> Up from down? Is Heaven's interface
>
> What your new friends tactfully don't call Hell?

Morse also is reported as criticizing the language of the spirit messages:

> . . . The real no-no
> Is jargon, falling back on terms that smell
>
> Just a touch fishy when the tide is low:
> 'Molecular structures'—cup and hand—obey
> 'Electric waves'? Don't *dream* of saying so!

But the New Age jargon of the transcripts goes on relentlessly. Even worse, after Robert Morse's death his ghost, according to the Ouija board, becomes a true believer, though he is definitely not on a high plane and for a long while cannot enter the schoolroom.

As the lessons continued, Jimmy was sometimes bored or impatient, but for him there were compensations: he was receiving the raw material for a major poem. And by the end of *Sandover* he seems to have totally accepted the supernatural system, at least as a metaphor:

> Beneath my incredulity
> All at once is flowing
> Joy, the flash of the unbaited hook—
> *Yes, yes, it fits, it's right, it had to be!*

David, on the other hand, remained uneasy, as he revealed later to Sandy McClatchy:

I remember, I was the first one to get kind of irritated that we were always dragging that board out. . . .

I remember thinking, if this is *us* doing it, what a hideous kind of schizophrenia as it were, with time just disappearing.

And the idea that I'd spend those hours at a ouija board seemed to me obscene; what a way to spend time, you know. That was before we got on to the Lessons, when it seemed that we were summoned to something. And then another feeling took over, the feeling of it being very, very egocentric, the idea that we were supposed to be taking and delivering these great messages. That seemed to me really bizarre and vain and bogus. It was the hardest thing to take. . . .

It immediately stopped being somewhat enjoyable and just became a big chore, one that didn't end till the Epilogue.

For months on end the spirits demanded a long daily session, first in Stonington and then in Athens; time that might have been spent more enjoyably was sacrificed to the project. Jimmy and David's spirit companion Maria declares in the poem that in the supernatural world self-sacrifice is a high good, that "TO BE USED HERE IS THE TRUE PARADISE." But David continued to have doubts.

Quite often, it struck me as, This is really very beautiful and lovely, you know, and it just misses Mary Baker Eddy by inches, and what in God's name are we doing on a bright, sunny day like this listening to this stuff. And it did seem to me nearly laughable. I remember little waves of embarrassment, that two supposedly intelligent adults were doing this.

Wading through page after page of complex spiritual lessons from imaginary beings, even though they are sometimes interrupted by Jimmy's and David's own real voices, can also cause embarrassment and doubt in a reader. But I gave *Sandover* the benefit of this doubt at first, though as Jimmy himself remarks in the poem:

. . . one benefit of doubt,
As of credulity, is its tiresomeness.

Besides, I recognized the theoretical attraction to a writer of systems, both natural and supernatural. Even if they are flawed or incomplete, they can help to order a chaotic universe. It doesn't matter if they're only half believed in: they can still produce and shape fiction and poetry.

In practice, the system that lay behind a work of art could be magical or scientific—it didn't matter. When I was writing *The War Between the Tates* I studied astrology in order to create a character who was a professional astrologer. I learned to cast horoscopes and provided them for most of my family and friends, including Jimmy and David. As a system, astrology is attractive because it orders the world, but not in a wholly rigid manner. Every horoscope and every human being is unique, but we are predisposed to have certain characteristics; we are "born that way," as popular genetics would put it. Most charts are so complex, however, that they lend themselves to many different interpretations.

Struck by the possibilities, I assigned a Sun sign to each of the four principal characters in *The War Between the Tates*, though I did not cast their horoscopes. I could then read off their Sun-sign personalities from my astrology textbook, which was amusing and saved a certain amount of time. On the other hand, it was also limiting.

Because I had also used a supernatural system as a basis for writing, I was initially tolerant of Jimmy's use of the Ouija board; I assumed he didn't take it all that seriously. But as time passed, I began to feel that the whole thing was going on too long and becoming more than a little scary. The Ouija-board spirits began to remind me too much of the vampire in one of Jimmy's early poems, "A Narrow Escape," who calls herself "a symbol of the inner / Adventure." Like Mirabell, she is compared to a bat, and Jimmy speaks of her "nightly / Drainings of one's life, the blood, the laugh." I thought at the time that I had politely concealed my doubts and fears, but evidently not: in *The Book of Ephraim* Jimmy speaks of my suppressed critical reaction as "Alison's shrewd / Silence."

From the beginning I didn't care for Ephraim. He was a part of David and Jimmy I hadn't met head-on before, and instantly felt estranged from. He was foreign, frivolous, intermittently dishonest, selfishly sensual, and cheerfully, coldly promiscuous. Nevertheless, I was flattered when Jimmy and David offered to consult Ephraim and find out where I was in the spiritual scheme and whom I had been in my last life. It turned out that I was on a rather low level: stage two, I think. (David and Jimmy had already attained level five.) In my last incarnation, I had been a nineteenth-century English spinster missionary named Helena Pons-Toby who was sent to Africa to convert the heathen. After a while the heathen found her so annoying that they murdered her.

Though I didn't let on, I was deeply upset by this information. What it meant to me was that in spite of their affectionate kindness and generous hospitality, something in David's and/or Jimmy's subconscious regarded me as an intellectually and spiritually low-level person. I felt that Helena Pons-Toby was a spiteful joke, a comment on my increasingly skeptical attitude towards Ephraim and the Ouija board, and also a threat.

Keep this up, it seemed to say, and the savages in us will become deeply irritated. We will get rid of you, we will cut you out of our lives.

Possibly, in a sense, I deserved this warning. To criticize any creative enterprise in its early stages can be destructive. The artist must not be, as Jimmy put it early in *Ephraim*, too "tough- / Or literal-minded, or unduly patient / With those who were." Questioning the messages from the Ouija board, I became a kind of Helena Pons-Toby: a prudish, judgmental friend who could not be trusted with their innermost secrets.

9
___

Key West

✳

KEY WEST in the late 1970s, when Jimmy and David first went to live there in the winter, was still a little-known, cut-rate paradise. It was full of small shops and sagging gingerbread cottages, unpaved streets and untrimmed bushes and trees. But it was below the frost line, and was warm and beautiful all winter long. Houseplants that cowered indoors up North grew four to six feet tall and mutated into strange jungle forms: begonias choked backyards, philodendrons climbed trees and put out foot-long heart-shaped leaves striated in waxy yellow and green. Back then there wasn't much traffic: the loudest sound after midnight was the crowing of the insomniac Key West roosters and an occasional screeching, snarling fight between wild six-toed cats descended from the ones Ernest Hemingway had owned.

Key West was originally David's idea, as Jimmy remarks in a poem called "Clearing the Title."

> . . . god help us, you
> Have chosen, sight unseen, this tropic rendezvous
> Where tourist, outcast, and in-groupie gather
> Island by island, linked together,
> Causeways bridging the vast shallowness—

But the choice was not all that odd: for decades the island had been a cold-weather retreat for writers. Hemingway and Frost and Stevens and Elizabeth Bishop were gone; but John Brinnin, John Ciardi, Barbara Deming, Ralph Ellison, John Hersey, Richard Wilbur, and Tennessee Williams still wintered there. All of them already were, or soon became, good friends of David and Jimmy. Key West was also notoriously welcoming to eccentrics and homosexuals: there were several gay guesthouses and bars, and it was common to see two men or two women holding hands or kissing on the street.

In the winter of 1978–79 David and Jimmy rented a

two-room cinder-block house on Whitehead Street. Their landlord was a friend called James Boatwright who lived in the other, smaller half of the house during the winter term. He was a part-time professor at Washington and Lee, an occasional poet, and the gifted editor of the literary magazine *Shenandoah*. He was friendly, courteous in a slow southern way, and notably easygoing—perhaps too easygoing. In appearance he was athletic and bluntly handsome; he was one of the first men I knew to adopt what was presently to be known as the gay clone look: tanned, well-muscled from frequent visits to a gym, with a Mexican-bandit mustache and semicowboy or semilumberjack clothes: plaid shirts, cutoff jeans, black or white T-shirts with the sleeves ripped off.

※

Jimmy and David were drawn to Key West in part by their growing disillusion with Athens. Already in August of 1978, announcing his return to New York that fall, David had written:

> I'm going to search for an ideal SOUTHERN site to build our Old Age solar house + veg garden. We keep feeling Greece (anyway Athens) is near an end. (August 11, 1978)

Every year the city was more crowded with traffic and tourists, they told me; the air was brown and poisonous with pollution. Several people in their circle, including their closest Greek friend, Maria Mitsotáki, had died. Their young lovers had grown up and moved into adult lives. David's boyfriend George was now an officer in the Greek merchant marine. Jimmy's boyfriend Strato, whom he had once compared to a statue of Apollo, had become an overweight, self-important young man with an awful mustache and a callous attitude towards women.

Moreover, David's fear of flying had increased to the point that getting to Athens meant a laborious week-long voyage by ship and train, involving discomfort, boredom, and seasickness. Once he had reached Athens he was reluctant to leave. Jimmy, however, still traveled often by air, giving readings and lectures and attending conferences all over the world, and sometimes returning to Stonington to write in solitude for weeks or months. The move to Key West brought their lives back together again, at least in the beginning.

*

I came to Key West for the first time in January 1979, staying for two weeks in Jim Boatwright's cottage while

Jimmy and David were away. When I returned in March with Edward Hower, who would become my second husband, David had just bought a big old house on Elizabeth Street. "We must all move here," he and Jimmy declared; but when David took me to see his purchase I was appalled. The lot was large, and in the historic zoned district known as Old Town; but it was on the edge of a dangerous, run-down area, and the building was a dark, filthy ruin. The kitchen especially horrified me: it was a mass of rotting floorboards, walls caked with dirt and grease, and exposed rusty plumbing. "I know it looks bad, but it's going to be beautiful," David assured me. I politely said nothing, but the project seemed hopeless.

I was wrong about 702 Elizabeth Street. Though the process of renovation was expensive—"The little green house . . . is costing a MINT—whole rear end rotten," Jimmy wrote me that summer (July 14, 1979)— a year later it had been transformed. A wide hallway led from the front door to a big sitting room and the sunlit garden beyond. The rooms were not large, but as in Stonington, everything in them was, according to William Morris's dictum, either useful or beautiful or both. Many objects were also slightly strange: the nineteenth-century comically melodramatic painting of buxom mermaids and mermen over the big white wicker sofa; the statuettes of Indian gods and demons; the patchwork crazy quilt on the guest room bed, part silk and part tweed; the canvas-curtained outdoor dining room, its roof trellis spilling pale-blue flowering vines; the little boomerang-shaped swimming pool. Across the pool, against the back fence, David later installed, at a slight slant, a huge mirror surrounded by exotic plants, which reflected the magical outdoor parties he and Jimmy had begun to give.

The move to 702 Elizabeth Street was the beginning of what seemed a renewed time of happiness for both David and Jimmy: a second chance, one recognized also by the Ouija board. In the summer of 1979, with the encouragement of the spirits, they celebrated their silver anniversary on the terrace of their Athens house. (In fact, they had been together twenty-four years, not twenty-five, but the date was correct according to Greek custom.) The ceremony as described in *Sandover* is moving. As instructed by the spirits, they cut a white lily, lit a candle, filled bowls with ice and salt, and listened to Strauss's *Rosenkavalier*. They renewed their commitment to each other and received blessings and congratulations from almost the whole supernatural cast of characters. David gave Jimmy a ring, and Jimmy responded:

Key West

It is an instant, lifelong amulet.
. . . I've no gift but these lines the years
Together write upon my face and yours.

Back in Key West later that year David was absorbed
in the remodeling and furnishing of the new house. As
a good amateur carpenter, he did some of the work
himself. He was proud and occupied and content—
though often there was some practical frustration or
delay to complain of or laugh at, since the plumbers
and electricians of Key West were notoriously casual.
Jimmy set up his typewriter in one of the tiny, book-
crammed studies he liked, this one with a red-flowering
hibiscus outside the window. The third volume of *Sandover*, *Scripts for the Pageant*, and its final coda, *The Higher
Keys*, with its farewell to the spirits of the Ouija board,
would be written there.

I too had fallen in love with the island, and in March
1979 I bought a much smaller house and began to spend
part of every winter there. One of the strongest attrac-
tions of Key West for me was the presence of David
and Jimmy. For years I hadn't seen them often enough,
and this was especially true of David, who spent so
much time in Greece. Friendship is hard to sustain over
great distances: it grows thin, centered on letters and
memories. Now we would be within walking distance

for part of every year. Since they stayed longer in Key West than I could, I depended on them for local news when I was away. David also generously found time to watch over the work being done on my cottage, and reported to me by mail and phone.

Key West was a good place to be in those years. The package tourists and cruise ships had not yet discovered it, and the streets were not jammed with traffic. The island was full of interesting people, many of them writers. During the day everyone worked, or pretended to, but in the evenings there were dinners and parties and visits to restaurants—most of them, back then, casual and cheap. There were always houseguests to meet, new books to borrow, and manuscripts to read. Soon Jimmy joined the weekly game of anagrams organized years before by John Ciardi, John Hersey, and Dick Wilbur, and still running today.

I spoke to Jimmy and David almost every day, and was often invited over to admire David's latest improvement or purchase, or hear the latest gossip. When Jimmy and I were both in town we used to swim in the half-deserted pool of a local southern grande dame called Floy Thompson. Floy was too elderly and ill to use the pool herself in the cool winter months, but she had generously given several friends keys to the green gate on Grinnell Street.

Like Floy's house, the pool had been built just after World War II. A big pool house ran along the street side, with a central sitting room and bar, and dressing rooms and baths at either end. Because they had been constructed long before mosquito control, both pool and pool house were enclosed in a tall cage of wire netting. Inside the cage were many exotic, slightly dangerous-looking flowering shrubs in huge painted pots: hibiscus and croton and crown of thorns, as well as a flock of white-painted metal and glass outdoor furniture.

Just outside the enclosure was an orchard of mango and papaya and sour orange and Key lime trees, and an orchid house where a hundred or more plants waited in the warm, slatted shade. When the fruit was ready to eat, or the orchids about to bloom, Floy's gardener brought them indoors. But he did not always come on time, and often the coarse crabgrass was littered with leaves and fallen overripe oranges.

Once the pool must have been very grand, but now the paint and webbing of the furniture was bleached and worn, the imported Mexican tiles chipped and cracked. There was supposed to be a pool service, but often when we arrived twigs and dead bugs floated in the water, and the corners of the pool enclosure were full of rustling dry leaves. Rusted sections of wire netting drooped high overhead, and the pool house was always locked and empty. In the right-hand dressing room three of Floy's elegant wide-brimmed straw and canvas hats still hung on the wall, but their pink ribbons and artificial pansies and roses, like her own hair, had faded almost to white.

The pool was over thirty feet long, and abruptly deep. You had to be careful to stay close to one side or the other, because at the far end a lichened faucet, once part of a fountain, hung out over the water, and if you came up under it you could crack your head. Jimmy and I both made that mistake. Sometimes the pool was heated, sometimes not; but by noon the sun had usually warmed it, though in January the depths could be icy.

Usually we swam laps, and then lay in the speckled sun for half an hour or so. Jimmy was still marvelously skillful in the water: he had an efficient splashless crawl, and a fast, elegantly windmilling backstroke. Wiry, thin, tanned, his hair dark with water, he would climb out of the pool on his narrow, high-arched bony feet, wearing dark green or dark red bathing shorts. As we lay on adjacent chaise longues we would exchange news and gossip, talk about books we'd read and films we'd seen, and sometimes about what we were writing.

If she were well enough we might later visit Floy Thompson in her pale shadowy orchid-crammed parlor. She received us in printed-chiffon dressing gowns and gold-strapped sandals, with the light behind her filtered through half-transparent ruffled curtains. Floy had been a great beauty, as a portrait over the sofa and many photos in silver frames proved. Now her hair was frozen into a mass of white cobweb curls, but her great dark eyes were still bright in her powdered, crumpled face.

Floy, who all her life had preferred men to women, brightened up wonderfully when Jimmy appeared. With her he assumed a confidential, courtly, almost flirtatious manner, and his voice slowed to a southern drawl. He always had a story for her, a reminiscence, a bit of news, often about someone I didn't know. Floy would lean towards him, giggling like a girl, while her maid brought us tall glasses of oversweetened iced tea with fresh mint. "Come again, real soon," she would tell him when we left, holding out a white, ringed hand. Once, in a gesture that was only half-mocking, he bent and kissed it.

10

Trouble

＊

WHEN DID IT ALL BEGIN to go bad, slowly at first and then faster and faster? Visibly, to me at least, in the winter of 1982–83. *Sandover* had been completed and published. Messages from the other world would still be sought and received occasionally, but the greater gods and ghosts had fallen silent.

David had become impatient with the process long before Jimmy did: more than once in previous years he told me that he was "sick and tired of the Ouija Board." Recently he had seemed tired in another sense: emotionally and even physically exhausted after a long session, so that he often slept until noon the next day. As he told Sandy McClatchy:

> I was always wanting to get it over with, and to move toward the end. . . . And I remember those times I'd feel really fatigued. And I did have a sense a lot of times that it was draining something away that we shouldn't be so wasteful about.

Yet though he seemed aware of how much of his life and energy he had given to the spirits, he would also sometimes claim that the sacrifice had been worth making.

It is no wonder that David felt both exhaustion and regret. For over twenty years he had provided at least half of the material for Jimmy's epic poem. With the skill of a novelist he had helped to create dozens of original characters, an elaborate plot, and a fantastic history and coşmology. Jimmy—and the spirits—were aware of this: in a 1981 interview he remarked:

> According to Mirabell, David is the subconscious shaper of the message itself, the "Hand" as they call him . . . while I'm the "Scribe," the one in whose words and images the message gets expressed. . . .

The transcripts as they stand could never have come into being without him. I wonder if the trilogy shouldn't have been signed with both our names— or simply "by DJ, as told to JM"?

But when *Sandover* appeared the following year, the only name on the title page was his own. Nothing came of the suggestion, and critics, to a man (and they are almost all men), have usually written and spoken as if *Sandover* were the work of James Merrill alone.

In any case, by 1982 the intensity of the Ouija board connection was over. David and Jimmy had broken the mirror through which the spirits ostensibly saw them: they were no longer visible to their supernatural interlocutors, no longer intimately joined by a transcendental teacup. Already, for many years, they had not been physically intimate. Instead they had engaged in brief affairs (David's far more numerous and more brief) with others. In Jimmy's case these others now tended to be sensitive, well-educated young men who liked poetry. In David's case they were usually tough, ill-educated young men who liked change and adventure. It was, I once thought, as if each were choosing temporary companions who exaggerated their differences, the differences that had once attracted them to each other. Jimmy's boyfriends were crude versions of himself as a troubled young aesthete; David's were crude versions of himself as a strong, handsome, restless young drifter.

For years Jimmy and David had accepted the temporary presence in each other's lives of these minor characters. Now, however, strains began to show. Essentially, Jimmy was a romantic. He often fell in love with the people he slept with; at the very least, he was likely to care for them deeply and want to get to know them intimately. Even in Greece he had been unable to take Ephraim's advice to love casually, and his young boyfriend, Strato, had caused him years of passion and grief.

David, on the other hand, was a sensualist. His attitude to physical love, like that of some other men I have known, not all of them homosexual, was that of a gourmet. If you look at the sexual life this way, you will be excited and pleased to discover the erotic equivalent of a new restaurant, or a new dish. You may enjoy it tremendously, but you won't want to go back to the same place night after night; you'll want to try other restaurants, other new dishes. You will search for variety: French, Italian, Greek, Japanese, Mexican, Near Eastern. You may also, as David did, purchase gourmet magazines that feature a variety of delicious-looking bodies. He once showed me some of these magazines, which were full of spotlit soft-porn photos of beautiful, rather stupid-looking young men. I didn't like them, or the idea of them. He knew this, of course, though I didn't say so.

One warm, windy day in the early 1980s, when Jimmy was briefly out of town, David and I had lunch in their garden, in the half-sun, half-shade of an arbor entwined with flowers. As we finished our chicken and avocado salad, David explained to me that though he no longer wanted to sleep with Jimmy, it irritated him that Jimmy should care for anyone else seriously. After all, none of his own short-lived connections could compete for a moment with what he felt for Jimmy.

Why couldn't Jimmy just enjoy sex casually, aesthetically? he asked. That was what he did—most recently, I knew, with young working-class men who thought of themselves as straight, but were willing to make themselves available for a quid pro quo: a good meal, a sharp new outfit, a small "loan." The idea of sex as a financial transaction did not embarrass David; after all, one expects to pay well for a good dinner.

I looked down into my iced mint tea as he spoke, to conceal my reaction to this well-argued position, and did not comment. Commercial sex seemed to me corrupt, low-grade, humiliating. How could anyone want to sleep with persons who wouldn't even touch you unless they were paid to do so? I didn't say this, but David, perceptive as ever, must have intuited it. For this conversation was, I realized later, the end of my real friendship with him. Afterwards, whenever we were alone together, David was, as I wrote in my journal, "cozy without being confidential, and though witty and pleasant, withdrawn. We are not going to speak intimately ever again, his agreeable manner somehow says."

＊

It was perhaps naive of me to disapprove of David's sexual life. After all, Jimmy had more options. Though he was now over fifty, because of his fame he still attracted many possible lovers. These young men did not want money: what they wanted was to be the official boyfriend of a well-known writer. In the early 1980s this role was filled by a shy, agreeable youth who owned an organic orchard in northern New England. He loved poetry and Jimmy, but his first loyalty was to his hilly acres of apple trees. He visited Stonington in the summer, and came to Key West for a week or two every winter; but, like all farmers, he could not leave his land for long. His connection with Jimmy wasn't central to either of their lives, and though it might irritate David, it did not deeply disturb him.

*

Meanwhile, in Key West, practical problems were developing. Since buying the house on Elizabeth Street, David had become more and more involved with his poorer neighbors. He called on them, listened to their many troubles, and did his best to help them. In 1983, for instance, he paid to have the tumbledown shack across the street, which belonged to an old black man, equipped with electricity and hot water; he also had the house painted—to improve his own view, some ill-wishers said. Characteristically, David admitted to this motive, and even used it as an excuse for his generosity.

At the same time, he also began to befriend local young men, usually black, who had problems with drink and drugs and violent behavior and often had been in trouble with the law. No matter what the charge, David insisted that his protégés had been wrongly accused and mistreated by the system. He heard their hard-luck stories, lent them money, found them lawyers, paid their bills, and signed their bail bonds when they were arrested for drug possession or theft. If bail was denied, he visited them in jail.

Unfortunately, many of these young men did not reciprocate David's good will. They skipped bail and left town; they hung around the house on Elizabeth Street, flashily or shabbily dressed. They played loud music and drank and smoked grass, and sometimes used harder drugs. When two or more of them were present, they occasionally had quarrels marked by cursing and shoving. Some of them also began to steal from David, and from Jimmy. Small change slipped off dressers and shirts from hangers; small bills vanished from wallets.

David's response was to pretend that these things had not happened ("He didn't take it; I gave it to him") or that objects had been misplaced ("You know you're always forgetting where you put your watch"). Jimmy disputed these claims. He argued with David, trying to persuade him to keep his more disreputable friends and lovers out of the house, or at least to watch them more carefully.

David then became sulky. He blamed Jimmy for leaving cash and valuables around; if somebody was broke and needy, naturally it was a temptation—even a kind of entrapment. His friends had been the victims of prejudice and poverty all their lives; if they helped themselves to a dollar here and there, so what? He and Jimmy could afford it, for Christ's sake.

All right, David agreed impatiently. If that was what Jimmy wanted, he wouldn't leave his visitors alone in the house. But by this time, somehow, more than one of David's protégés had acquired keys. One morning when I stopped by without calling first, as I had often done in the past, the door was opened by a half-dressed, sullenly embarrassed black teenager in stained yellow silk underpants who mumbled that Jimmy was out and David still in bed. I never visited again at any time of the day without phoning first.

In the early 1980s such scenes were still infrequent. For a while there were periods of peace and stability, often when David's latest young friend was in jail. Then there were lunches in the garden with shrimp bisque and fresh Key West yellowtail and jokes and gossip; dinner parties with duets on the piano and Jimmy's homemade chocolate mousse, when it seemed like old times. And of course there were still the pleasant summers in Stonington.

As David's protégés became more numerous, he began to spend more time in Key West: to arrive early in October and remain until June. Jimmy had now taken over his mother's apartment in Manhattan, and often stayed there for a few days when he flew to the city on business. But David did not fly, and there was less to attract David in New York, where only a few friends remembered the brilliance and wit of his published stories and unpublished novels.

Eventually Jimmy gave up trying to keep David's protégés out of the house. ("I can't do anything about it," he told me one day, sitting on the edge of Floy's pool and weeping into the water.) Instead he began to spend less and less time in Key West—to arrive later in the winter and leave earlier, to travel more and accept more invitations to give readings and lectures all over America and abroad. And there were more such invitations now. By the mid-1980s Jimmy's poems were in many anthologies, and his books had won all the most important literary prizes. He had, as he had predicted nearly thirty years before while making a tomato salad, become a famous person.

11

Peter

✳

THE MOST IMPORTANT BY-PRODUCT of Jimmy's fame and his expanded lecture schedule—one that would affect his life profoundly—was a tall, handsome young actor called Peter Hooten, a former featured player in several B-list Hollywood films whose greatest success, according to some of Jimmy's friends, had been in the low-budget Italian cowboy epics known as "spaghetti Westerns." These films would have been an ideal showcase for Peter's particular talents. Since the voices were dubbed in Italian, it was not necessary for the actors to have outstanding dramatic ability: what counted were good looks, athletic energy, and physical grace.

Peter

Though he had not graduated from, or possibly even attended, college, Peter Hooten was, or aspired to be, a highly cultured person. He revered poetry, especially the work of James Merrill. That was how they met in 1984: Peter approached Jimmy after a reading at UCLA, presenting a volume of poems for an autograph. Not long afterwards he appeared at another, similar occasion in New York with several more books to be signed. He had read everything Jimmy had ever written, he declared; he was Jimmy's greatest fan.

A few days later Jimmy received a letter from Peter, enclosing a large, glossily sexy publicity photograph. He was sending this photo, Peter said, to help Jimmy recall their meeting. He had a great favor to ask: could they possibly get together, perhaps over drinks, to discuss it? What he wanted, he said, was permission to perform James Merrill's poems in public, at a time and place to be arranged. He would like so much to tell Mr. Merrill more about this project, and ask his advice. Like most famous writers, Jimmy had now become somewhat wary of fans who wanted something. He showed the letter and photo to his friend Sandy McClatchy. What should he do? "Hey, go for it," Sandy said.

※

It is difficult to know what Peter Hooten looked and sounded like at those first critical meetings, since by the time I and most of Jimmy's friends met him he was on his way to becoming a kind of clone of the poet he admired so much. Soon he had shaved off his spaghetti-Western beard, and wore his dark, curly hair in a close-cut crop with short floppy bangs like Jimmy's. He began to dress like Jimmy, in simple, expensive, well-cut clothes of subtle, unexpected hues: lavender and sea-green cotton sweaters, blush-pink and sand-beige open-neck shirts. Like Jimmy, he wore Birkenstock sandals or Japanese straw flip-flops. Many of these items, it appeared, were gifts from his beloved.

Peter also began to walk like Jimmy, in a kind of slow glide, and to imitate Jimmy's gestures, notably his habit of clasping his hands round one slightly lifted knee. He voiced Jimmy's opinions and tastes, with considerably more vehemence and solemnity than their originator. What is more, he began to express these views in an approximation of Jimmy's voice: the distinctive drawl, half southern and half upper-class Long Island, that reflected Jimmy's childhood in Florida and New York and his youth in expensive eastern schools and colleges. The impersonation was sometimes spookily good; but of course Peter was an actor—a better actor perhaps than his past career had suggested.

At first, Jimmy's delight in his new love, his happiness and his evident affection for Peter, touched his friends, and we were cordial. But it was not long before some of us began to have reservations. Peter's lack of humor—let alone of Jimmy's subtle, glancing, affectionate irony—was a problem. His increasingly close imitation of Jimmy's dress, speech, gestures, manners, and opinions also made us uneasy. Who was Peter Hooten, beneath this impersonation? According to one report, he had been born and raised in central Florida, in modest circumstances.

Whatever Peter Hooten was or had been, he was also now in a sense the incarnation of those spirits and demigods who had spoken to Jimmy and David through the Ouija board. Like Ephraim, he was unusually beautiful, if you admire that sort of thing. And like the spirits, he held Jimmy in the highest esteem, proclaiming him a gifted, enlightened, and superior being—superior indeed to almost everyone now on Earth.

It is this above all, perhaps, that explains Jimmy's attachment to him. Imagine that, for over twenty years, disembodied spirits have told you repeatedly that you are brilliant and perfect. Then suppose that these spirits suddenly fall silent. Even if you have banished them yourself, isn't it likely that you will be happy to hear this sort of praise and declaration of unqualified love again? Most human beings, however, even if they are in love with you, will eventually have some reservations, some minor criticisms. They will also wish you to admire them as much as they do you. Moreover, they will not always be available when you want them: sometimes they will be busy pruning and grafting apple trees, for instance.

Peter Hooten admired Jimmy as uncritically as the spirits of the Ouija board—and, like them, he was always available. Up to now, all Jimmy's previous lovers, even if they wanted to share Jimmy's life for a while, also had lives of their own. What Peter Hooten wanted, it was becoming more and more clear, was Jimmy's life.

Some people who thought well of Peter said that naturally, like many actors, he seemed a little unreal and unfocused offstage. For an actor, they said, it was an advantage to have no strong, definite personality or manner, to be able to take on whatever role presented itself. Or perhaps, they suggested, Peter was so infatuated with Jimmy that he didn't realize that he was imitating him.

To other people, though, Peter's increasing use of the

royal We ("We rather liked that film") seemed presumptuous; his tendency to speak for his famous new friend oppressive. Most disturbing of all was his growing omnipresence, which made it difficult to maintain even the most long-standing friendship with Jimmy. One Key West acquaintance, frustrated by this, compared Peter to the remora, a parasitic tropical fish that had been the subject of one of Jimmy's early poems. The remora clings to much larger fish by means of a suction disk, getting free meals and a free ride. As for the larger fish, as Jimmy put it presciently,

When chosen they have no defense—. . .
And where two go could be one's finer sense.

Another problem was something that had pleased many of us at first: Peter's reverent admiration for his beloved. In Peter's view, Jimmy was not like other men and women; he was a great poet, a genius. Yes, that's right, we said, smiling. But then came a time when Peter sought out several of Jimmy's oldest friends individually to suggest that we did not seem to be sufficiently aware of his greatness. For example, he said that it was really somewhat discourteous and overfamiliar of us to call him "Jimmy." It would be more appropriate for us to address him, especially in public, as "James," the way Peter always did. Naturally, this suggestion did not go over very well.

*

But the most disturbing aspect of Peter Hooten's appearance on the scene was its effect on David. Unlike the spirits, Peter did not regard David Jackson as a beautiful and enlightened and superior being. Rather, from Peter's point of view, David was an unattractive, useless, aging, inconvenient person who had never accomplished anything; who drank too much and brought criminal creeps into James Merrill's precious life.

Some of Jimmy and David's friends looked at all this from another point of view. David's protégés certainly caused trouble, but all they really wanted was a little money, and sometimes a place to sleep. Besides, they were never around for long: they skipped bail and left town, or were sent to jail. They didn't threaten David's long-standing relationship to Jimmy; they could not alter it. As David once told me, he didn't really care about any of these boys, though they could be fun for a while. "Mostly," he said, "the next morning I just want to get them out of the house as fast as possible."

Of course, it wasn't always so easy to get them out of the house. Sometimes they hung about sulkily, wanting to borrow money, wanting a beer or some grass or something to eat. Still, usually they were gone before lunch.

Peter was different: it was clear after a while that he meant to stay around as long as possible; that he wanted Jimmy and Jimmy's love all to himself, and was jealous of his beloved's other ties. From David's point of view this was the last straw. He began to tell friends that Peter, though he might resemble a Greek statue, was a false copy; he was a phony and a parasite. He was also, David believed, after Jimmy's money, and in a big way. He didn't just need a few dollars for groceries or a hundred for a lawyer; he wanted the Merrill fortune.

Perhaps because Peter was always there, David stopped making much effort to get rid of his own temporary boyfriends, or to monitor their behavior. Some people even speculated that he was encouraging them to hang around and cause trouble for Jimmy and Peter. Whatever the truth of this, it was apparent that David's protégés were now more visible and more objectionable, and that larger and more valuable things were beginning to disappear from the cottage on Elizabeth Street: radios and tape recorders; eventually the hi-fi and the television set.

After each disappearance there were bitter quarrels. Finally Jimmy had locks installed on the doors to his

Key West bedroom and study. But even this was ineffective: one evening when the house was empty someone forced the study door, splitting and splintering the wood. As David insisted later, it could have been a complete stranger. But in any case Jimmy's new laptop computer was gone, along with everything on his hard drive, including drafts of two new poems.

By the end of the 1980s tension between Peter and David had escalated to the point that it was difficult for them to be in the same room. In January 1990 Jimmy told me that Peter would only be coming back to Key West briefly. "He feels unwelcome here," Jimmy said. "He thinks people don't like him." I could not reassure him on this point, and a silence followed, broken only by the raucous crowing of one of Key West's confused roosters.

"Anyhow," Jimmy resumed, "it's probably a good thing for Peter to be in New York, so he can work on his projects." "Oh yes," I agreed, incurious about these projects, and pleased to think that now I and Jimmy's other friends would get to see him alone.

For a while our hopes were fulfilled; there were many happy lunches and dinners and excursions, unencumbered by Peter's watchful solicitude. But back in the city Peter grew lonely and restless. For a long time he had asked nothing more than to be near Jimmy and worship him. Now that he couldn't express his love in person he became sulky and sad. He began to make demands, to put pressure on Jimmy to return to New York, or find some place to stay in Key West that wasn't David's house.

In public, at least, Peter and David still treated each other with a flat, restrained politeness; but their true feelings were clear. It was not long before everyone recognized that they were engaged in a life-and-death struggle for the possession of James Merrill's time, attention, and love. Watching the contest, most of us—but not all—were backing David. It didn't occur to anyone that all three could lose.

It would be a long battle. Though Jimmy and David's relationship was strained now and marked by bitter altercations and even more bitter silences, they still had much in common: over thirty years of shared memories, three shared houses, many shared friends, and their complex involvement with the spirits and gods of the Ouija board—the long intense intellectual and psychological adventure that had become *The Changing Light at Sandover*. Peter could do nothing about the memories or the houses, and he had by that time alienated most of Jimmy's friends. Instead, he turned his attention to *Sandover*.

12

Video Days

✳

NOT LONG AFTER THEY MET, Peter began to carry out his plan of performing Jimmy's poetry. He did not perform it alone, however: rather, he started to accompany Jimmy to poetry readings all over the country, and to appear on stage with him. At these events some of Jimmy's poems would be read by Jimmy; others would be read, much more dramatically, by Peter. (On occasion, Peter would also recite the work of other poets, notably Jimmy and David's friend Elizabeth Bishop, who was unable to challenge Peter's highly mannered reading because she had died in 1979.) Afterwards Jimmy would split the fee with Peter—a practical move, since Peter was no longer acting in films. To do so would have necessitated his returning to Italy, or moving to Los Angeles, and interfered with their close companionship.

After a while Peter began to read dramatic excerpts from *Sandover* at these events, speaking in the voices of the spirits who had spoken silently through the Ouija board. It was only a short step from this to his next project, which was to bring the whole work to a larger audience. It seemed a natural move—after all, *Sandover* was already almost a play: it had different characters, different voices, dramatic monologues and dialogues. Besides, the spirits had already showed their approval of performance: as Ephraim put it,

. . . SOME
FANS OF YOURS IN HEAVEN, A SMALL CROWD,
HAD HOPED TO HEAR THE POEM READ ALOUD.

What Peter wanted was to make a video of *Sandover*. He himself would produce, cast, direct, and star in this film, which would ultimately be financed through the sale of the resulting tapes. It would be shown on public TV first, Peter assumed; later copies would be sold to schools and colleges, where they would be used in courses on American poetry for years to come. Estimating future earnings, it did not seem unreasonable for him to ask Jimmy to make a considerable investment in the project. To keep everything official, Peter incorporated himself, with the help of a lawyer, as Peter Hooten Productions, Inc.

In the end, the video of *Sandover* would cost over $800,000. It was shown (without a fee) at a few colleges, but never purchased by any television station. Why this should have been so became clear in 1991, when Edward and I attended the Key West premiere of the program.

It took place on the evening of February 19, in David's garden. A large television was set up on a table by the pool, against a background of dimly spotlit flowers and leaves. The audience sat facing the screen in white plastic chairs, holding glasses—of champagne, for this was a premiere, a celebration. Many well-known people were present, including John Malcolm Brinnin, John and Barbara Hersey, and Dick and Charlee Wilbur, and others less well known but pleased and honored to be present at this historic literary occasion.

The video lasted two hours, and seemed to last longer. There were moments of relief, notably when Jimmy appeared on screen to read his own lines, and (as always) read them brilliantly. There were also moments of pretentious silliness, as when David and Jimmy's first supernatural contact, Ephraim, appeared in the shape of a blond pussycat-plump young man classically draped in a white sheet, reclining on top of what was obviously a nineteenth-century dining room sideboard. He was a professional actor, as was everyone in the video with the exception of Jimmy. Peter, perhaps appropriately, played Mirabell, who had first been described as a black bat and later been transformed into a peacock. On screen, however, his face emerged from a starburst of lighting effects, suggesting that he was a divine being, and he spoke in echoing elocutionary tones. Auden, Maria, and—worst of all—David Jackson were also played by actors selected by Peter. Meanwhile the real David sat in the shadows by the far wall, half concealed by a dark shrub. He did not, as some people might have done in his place, protest or walk out.

When the program was over, everyone was polite, even congratulatory, though I couldn't manage a more positive adjective than Jimmy's trademark "remarkable." I thought that the video of *Sandover* was both boring and embarrassing, that it had turned an intermittently fine poem into pretentious New Age nonsense. I also thought that it was cruel and frightening in its implications, one of which was that David, like Auden and Maria, was dead, or at least no longer existed in any real sense. I was frightened to see that Jimmy apparently accepted this travesty of his work as genuine, and was genuinely proud of Peter's effort—that he seemed unaware of the implied insult to David and its clearly destructive intent.

It was as if he had forgotten who David was, or rather who he had been. I remembered still, but I had to realize that not everyone did: that much of him was gone now. Over the last few years David had seemed to age more rapidly than normal, to take on a thin, bleached, frayed look, like something that has been left out too long on a clothesline, battered by sun and wind and rain. Jimmy, of course, had seen it first. "I can't take this," he had cried to me over the phone one day in December 1986, weeping in gulps, after a quarrel over something Peter had done or said to David, or vice versa—I couldn't get the story straight. "David's so blurry and forgetful, he doesn't realize, he doesn't think—he doesn't use his mind anymore. And you know, if you don't, it's like any muscle, it atrophies."

※

It was true that, at least on the surface, David had altered and blurred. What had happened to all that wit and brilliance and inventiveness? Perhaps too much of it had gone into the messages from the spirits, and the creation of a more and more fantastic world system.

But now that the connection with the spirits was over, much of David's wit and inventiveness seemed to have gone, too, as if, as he had said, something in him had been drained dry. His creative energy showed itself only intermittently, in proposals for work other people might write. I remember especially the plots of a mystery for the children's author Steve Roos that never became a book, and a Key West ghost story that I eventually wrote in a different version.

Less happily, David's inventiveness had also begun to invade real life, and to expand and corrupt the stories he passed on about friends and acquaintances. He said that a beautiful young woman writer we all knew supported herself as a call girl; and that another acquaintance was a successful drug dealer. By the end of the 1980s, everyone in Key West knew that you couldn't always believe what David said. It was as if, in his increasingly blurred consciousness, his friends and acquaintances had become characters in fiction, or disembodied spirits, and therefore whatever he imagined about them might as well be true.

Even before the *Sandover* video it was clear that David had changed; that he was no longer the same person. For one thing, he had become a creature of the afternoon and night. While Jimmy, as always, liked to rise early and be in bed by eleven, David now stayed up long past midnight and slept late. He lit his first cigarette before he got out of bed, and had his first drink at lunch. Soon he was only fully clearheaded for a few hours at midday; after that he entered a blurry half-life, which his remaining intelligence and sophistication allowed him to disguise as boredom, careless insouciance ("Really, you know, I couldn't care less about that"), or laid-back good nature.

For most of his life David had been full of physical and intellectual energy, able to spend hours writing, painting, gardening, working on houses. Now he began to speak of himself as "lazy." In fact, he didn't seem lazy so much as depressed and exhausted.

Also, in the mid-1980s, David began to have a series of minor but painful illnesses: skin rashes, migraines, a sprained ankle. Jimmy realized what was happening long before the rest of us did. He tried to spend more time with David, to speak to him about books and current events. He attempted to interest him, with Barbara Hersey's help, in volunteer work in the community. ("He's so good with people, he could do something for someone who really needs help—in the local literacy program for instance," Jimmy explained to me. Instead, he didn't say, didn't have to say, of involving himself with hopeless low-life types.) These efforts were not well received. When I phoned one morning in December 1986 Jimmy answered. They had just had a bitter fight; David had rushed out of the house. Where was he now? Had he called me, had I seen him?

Jimmy at this time had not yet despaired of David. He worried about David's health, and nagged him until he went in for a checkup. It turned out that, having smoked heavily for over fifty years, David had developed emphysema; as the doctor explained, David's brain wasn't getting enough oxygen. A few days later two oxygen tanks, like tall brass rockets, appeared in the house on Elizabeth Street. When David breathed the gas, Jimmy reported, he was as alert and clearheaded as ever. "It's going to be all right," he told me euphorically.

The problem was that people who are on oxygen cannot smoke. Jimmy had given up cigarettes years before, but David even now failed to stop, or refused to stop. Possibly he did not wish to be alert and clearheaded. After a few fraught weeks the oxygen tanks were taken away, and he relapsed into a dazed and blurred mental condition.

At the premiere of the *Sandover* video the transformation of David was clear to everyone. It hadn't been Jimmy's fault, I thought later that night as I lay awake; but maybe there was something about Jimmy that had allowed it to happen: his unworldliness, his aesthetic detachment, his sense that words and ideas were realer than people.

*

Having created the film version of *Sandover*, Peter felt that he knew the work intimately. He began to have opinions about the poem, to interpret it to other, lesser fans. And as Peter grew more articulate, David fell silent. He ate almost nothing; he chain-smoked, and began drinking earlier. He spoke less and less, even to close friends. Soon after he rose, now never before noon, he would start sipping white wine, and continue until late at night. He read only the local paper now, and watched more and more daytime television. When Jimmy remonstrated with him about this, asking how he could stand hours and hours of soap operas every day, David replied, "I give them my life, and they give me their lives." As Jimmy repeated these words to me, I felt an involuntary shudder. That was what happened before, I thought, with the spirits that used the Ouija board. He gave them his life.

"He's disappearing, you know," Jimmy told me a few weeks after the *Sandover* premiere. "Sometimes now I recognize in him only his mother or father, one nervously compulsive, one impatient and irritable. . . . He's haunted by both his parents." "Well," I replied uneasily, "perhaps we all are, as we get older." Yes, Jimmy agreed; "and the less compatible they were, the stranger the effect."

"I think David wants to die," Jimmy said another day, as we sat by Floy's pool. "Or else it's just that he doesn't want to live anymore."

Yes, maybe so, I thought: or maybe he doesn't want to live in a world in which he is a failure and you are in love with Peter Hooten.

*

Even before the showing of the video, David had seemed to know what was coming. The next few years only made clear to everyone what had long been happening. After years of association with ghosts, David was turning into a ghost. Or perhaps it would be more accurate to say that he was turning himself into a ghost. Every year when I arrived in Key West I found him thinner, paler, and blurrier. His hair grew wispier and whiter, his manner vaguer, his wrinkled white shirts hung looser on his skeletal arms.

It was a process that would take a long time. As I write, it has been over nine years, and is still unfinished. When I last saw David, in March of 2000, he could only walk or speak with difficulty. He was supported from room to room, and cared for in every way, by two kind gay men called Rolando and John, who several years ago had moved into his house for this purpose.

It was unclear whether or not he really recognized me. For years his conversation had become more and more disjointed and evasive. His customary greeting, "Hello there, baby," now emerged as a kind of automatic croak, as if some child had pulled the string on an aged talking teddy bear.

13

Endings

✳

LIVING WITH SOMEONE ELSE, even someone you love, is never wholly easy. The beloved is sure eventually to reveal unfamiliar, even disturbing aspects: conflicting tastes, opinions, and desires. When he or she is of another generation, background, or temperament, the difficulties increase. But there is a silvery lining to this cloud of conflict. The greater the differences between yourself and the other, the more of the world you can potentially experience and understand.

Occasionally one sees couples who appear to share almost everything, and sometimes such people also resemble each other. They wear the same clothes, have the same haircuts, use the same slang. If they are both men, or both women, the illusion of identity can be even stronger. Within such couples, to love the other seems almost to love oneself. But even in these cases hidden disparities often appear eventually.

When Peter Hooten turned himself into a clone of Jimmy, he became lovable in the same way that some of the spirits of the Ouija board were lovable: as idealized selves and uncritical admirers. To be loved unconditionally by the spirits, David and Jimmy did not have to change or adapt. In the same way, Jimmy at first did not have to adapt to Peter; he could simply relax and sun himself in Peter's love.

But although Peter's feeling for Jimmy was fervent and genuine, he was not Jimmy or a supernatural manifestation of Jimmy. To become a clone, he necessarily had to suppress some part of himself. And as time passed, this suppressed self began to fight for expression. It was perhaps inevitable that this self was a Mr. Hyde to Peter's polite, cultured, serene public self, so much like Jimmy's. It was impulsive, unbalanced, violent, and greedy. It wanted different things. Jimmy, now in his mid-sixties, preferred to spend evenings at home reading, talking with friends, or listening to music, and to be in bed by eleven. Peter, who was over thirty years younger, wanted excitement and change. His suppressed self wanted to go drinking and dancing, and meet exciting, glamorous people. It wanted to stay out all night and have sudden, dramatic encounters. Sometimes, after Jimmy was asleep, it would leave the house and do so.

The results of Peter's solitary midnight excursions were, as usual in such cases, confrontation, anger, recrimination, guilt, tears, repentance, promises to reform. As strains in the relationship continued and escalated, experts were called in. Once they might have been ministers or priests. Now, of course, they were psychologists. In October 1991, over the phone, Jimmy revealed that Peter was "in a rehabilitation facility." Yes, it was necessary, he said when I asked. "He has a drinking problem, and he's been getting into cocaine."

Over the next few years many kinds of therapy and hospitalization followed: usually for Peter alone, but sometimes for both Peter and Jimmy. In the course of these treatments Peter was told, in the current jargon, that he was "acting out," that he had "a damaged inner child" and "problems with authority." Jimmy was told that he was an "enabler" and that there was a "co-dependency problem." It was not only that Peter was addicted to drink and drugs: he and Jimmy were addicted to each other. According to other experts Jimmy was partly or even largely to blame for Peter's problems.

With infinite patience and goodwill, Jimmy accepted or at least considered these interpretations. Over the next few years, Peter was in and out of various therapeutic relationships and facilities, notably a very expensive one in the Southwest where Jimmy joined him briefly, and about which he wrote one of his best late poems, "Family Week at Oracle Ranch." It catches the therapeutic jargon exactly, as well as reporting his own forbearance:

> Their ritualized responses serve the plot.
>
> Ken, for example, blond brows knitted: "When
> James told the group he worried about dying
> Without his lover beside him, I felt SAD."
> Thank you for sharing, Ken,
>
> I keep from saying; it would come out snide.

Though Jimmy was intermittently hopeful that Peter could be helped by therapy, the end of this poem, after a rundown of the Oracle Ranch prognosis of 40 percent recovery, is almost despairing:

> And if the old patterns recur?
> Ask how the co-dependent moon, another night,

Feels when the light drains wholly from her face.
Ask what that cold comfort means to her.

As yet, the darkest phase of the moon had not yet
come, though its shadow already hung over all of us. As
Jimmy and his contemporaries aged, as friends died—
some of them, like David Kalstone and Jim Boatwright,
of AIDS—we became more aware of our own mor-
tality. Already in February 1990, after a series of what
seemed minor ailments (flu, toothache, sinus infection),
Jimmy had remarked to me, laughing lightly, "I'm afraid
Death is beginning to be interested in me." Yes, that
was true of all of us, I said stupidly.

But for the next few years Jimmy seemed fairly well,
and he was far more often anxious about David's and
Peter's health than his own. In January 1993, for instance, when we were both in Key West, he called, half-
weeping, to tell me he couldn't go swimming that
afternoon; he'd just heard that Peter had been on a
four-day "bender" in New York, and he had to get on
the phone to people there.

A few days later we met at Floy's pool. Jimmy had
been ill again: a low-grade cold, he said. I accepted
this story, and put his pale, creased look down to con-
valescence and the strain of Peter's problems. Jimmy
was nearly sixty-seven, and after years of amazing

youthfulness his age showed when he wasn't well. But he was still a fast, skilled swimmer, and in the pool beautiful to watch, utterly at home in the long box of cool green water.

Things were better in New York, he told me; two doctors had checked Peter into a hospital, and he was doing well. It was David who was the problem now. He was still smoking and drinking heavily, and wouldn't stop, although he was coughing painfully and almost incoherent with alcohol by suppertime. And unlike Peter he wouldn't get professional help.

Jimmy couldn't take it, he said. He'd decided he couldn't live with David anymore. When I asked where he would live instead, he said he didn't know. "I don't want to live alone," he told me. "And Stonington, in the winter—" Yes, I agreed, that would be dreary.

"I've been used to going from one house to another where I am always welcomed, all my life," Jimmy said, with a short half-laugh. "But now . . ." Now, he didn't need to say, both the houses he might go to contained angry, troubled persons.

"I'm leaving the week after next," he revealed as we lay side by side in the winter sun on the worn outdoor furniture. "I probably won't be coming back here for long." It was the nearest he ever came to telling me that he was seriously ill. I didn't want to know the truth, and heard him wrong—I thought he only meant that he wouldn't be returning to Key West except for a short stay, which turned out to be true, too.

✳

But by the following winter there had been a change. It wasn't just Jimmy: Key West had changed too, I finally realized that year, and not for the better. It was no longer a little-known paradise for writers and artists. There were more tourists, more expensive motels and guesthouses, more T-shirt shops. Huge floating-hotel cruise ships had begun to dock, often blocking the sea view from Mallory Dock for most of the day.

The worst thing about it was that those of us who had recently discovered the island were guilty of these changes. Earlier winter residents had been more discreet; they might mention the island in a poem or a story, but they didn't write articles about it for glossy travel magazines and newspapers, as we naively did.

Slowly but relentlessly this publicity brought in more visitors and transformed Key West into a noisy, crowded, expensive resort town. The deserted navy base where many of us had rented sea-view studios for $50 a month became a gated community of expensive condominiums.

Faded palm-shaded cottages like the one I once bought for $40,000 were extensively remodeled and resold for $400,000.

The news that the island was full of writers and artists attracted the sort of people who like to know writers and artists, not all of them the sort of people writers and artists like to know. It also attracted other writers and artists, most of whom were welcomed by the older residents. But all these new arrivals had one thing in common: they were very well off. Commercial success, or inherited wealth, made it possible for them to pay the now-inflated rents and house prices. People who could not afford these prices stopped coming to Key West.

Jimmy too had changed. He seemed troubled and confused—and, worse, somehow damaged and diminished. By the strains of two difficult relationships, I thought. Or was it more than that? In January 1994, at a buffet dinner party given by Dick and Charlee Wilbur, he appeared late, looking ill and—very unusual for him—untidy, in shabby, ill-matched clothes. At one point he half-stumbled, half-fell over a stool, and spilt a sloppy plateful of salad on his wrinkled pink slacks.

"I'm worried about Jimmy," I said on the phone to Frank Taylor the next day. "What is the matter with him?" I wanted Frank to tell me that it was flu, or anxiety about David and Peter. Instead there was a silence. "He's sick," Frank said finally, slowly. He didn't have to name the disease.

*

But how did he catch it? people whispered as the news of Jimmy's illness passed among his friends and acquaintances. No one whispered the question to Jimmy, though, nor did he speak of having a serious illness. When he claimed to have some other, minor ailment, no one challenged him. With Sandy McClatchy, however, he was more frank. It was impossible to know where the virus came from, he told Sandy. He might, for instance, have picked it up from David Kalstone's razor while visiting his friend in New York years ago. Clearly, this was implausible: for one thing, if Jimmy needed a place to stay in New York he had the use— and from 1983 on, the full possession—of his mother's apartment on East Seventy-second Street; and he was far too fastidious ever to use anyone else's razor.

*

The last time I saw Jimmy was in the late fall of 1994. I didn't know it was the last time, didn't even consider the possibility. There were so many new treatments now, I thought, and many people were actually getting better.

We met in his mother's former apartment. For the first time, the large, elegantly decorated rooms (which had always reminded me of an expensive apartment-hotel) were darkened and untidy. The heavy Nile-green satin curtains were drawn, the bookshelves half-empty, the many little mahogany tables clumsily piled with magazines and papers. Jimmy, who claimed he had "a little cold," looked pale and tired, but not seriously ill. Peter Hooten was there, and so was the rather silly little white Jack Russell terrier called Cosmo that Jimmy had bought for Peter on the advice of one of their therapists, "so that he'll have something to take care of and be responsible for besides himself." Soon after I arrived, Jimmy asked Peter to take Cosmo out for a walk, to my relief. It was the first time in months we had been alone together.

Things were in disorder because they were packing for a winter visit to the Southwest, Jimmy explained. He was looking forward to the trip very much. Peter was much better in every way, and had been "wonderful" to him. I doubted this, but didn't question it. We spoke of friends, of a film they had seen—I don't remember which, so disappointed was I to learn that we wouldn't see each other in Key West that coming winter. When would we meet next? I wondered, and Jimmy said that he wasn't sure; his plans were unsettled. Then Peter and the silly dog returned, and I left.

*

A couple of months later, on February 6, 1995, Jimmy died suddenly in Tucson, Arizona. He had gone into the hospital a few days before with what seemed minor problems—at least, that was how it was described to us in Key West.

How could it have happened so fast, how could it be true? Over the phone lines, friends wept and wailed. Yet the *New York Times* obituary confirmed it: Jimmy was gone. For the first and only time, I wished that the supernatural world of *Sandover* were real, so that Jimmy could go on being himself somewhere.

But the event already had a supernatural aspect to it, as I learnt later: at the exact moment of Jimmy's death, David had called his hospital room in Arizona from Key West. I hope that this time Jimmy too had extrasensory perception, and knew who was on the phone.

14

Afterwards

✳

JIMMY'S DEATH was both the end, and not the end, of his life. Now, as Auden wrote of Yeats, he has become his admirers, and this process began almost at once. In the first years there were many memorial services, tributes and essays and articles, conferences and seminars on the work of James Merrill, and surely there will be more to come. At these events and in these writings almost no one mentioned David Jackson or Peter Hooten except in passing, though they, too, perhaps deserved to be mourned. Of course, technically they were not dead; but in an important sense their lives were over. David is now a ghost in Key West. Peter, according to report, is living a ghostly half-life of mourning in southern Florida; he was provided for generously in Jimmy's will, but most of Jimmy's share of the great Merrill fortune went to nonprofit institutions that support education and the arts.

✳

As time passed, some people blamed Peter for Jimmy's death, making several unfounded assumptions: that Peter was ill; that he knew he was ill; that, knowing he was ill, he did not tell Jimmy. Other people blamed David, for making life at home so wholly intolerable that Jimmy had been driven into Peter's arms.

Another way of looking at the catastrophe would be to say that the spirits of the Ouija board had destroyed all three of what were once, in different ways and to different degrees, beautiful and gifted young men. This was true of Peter, too: after all, if he hadn't tried so desperately to become first Jimmy, and then Jimmy's imaginary friend Mirabell, he might have continued to live out his natural life as a film and TV actor.

✳

One striking thing about Jimmy was that he never used his astonishing gifts to trumpet his own brilliance. On first reading, his work often seemed unassuming, even casual; only slowly did its wit, invention, and serious engagement with life appear. Even in his autobiography and in *Sandover*, he gave "JM" no special privileges, but turned his cool, amused, sometimes frighteningly penetrating gaze on himself as well as others. It was the same in real life: everything, even the lightest flicker of a match or a joke, might be serious—but nothing was ever solemn.

When I try to write about Jimmy's poetry, words fail me, except for his own. He is a ringmaster of language: alert to every possible twitch and roar. He must be one of the few poets who can successfully use words like "asymmetries," "X-raywise," and "oops!" in the same poem. In his work the flattest clichés are transformed into glowing images, and worn-out puns and similes catch fire. And, almost always, behind the flash and shimmer of language are denser meanings.

In the black light of Jimmy's death, many of his lines reverberate even more. In "Japan," for instance, he remarks that the New York clinic where a friend is dying is "vast and complex as an ocean liner." He goes on to speak of the passengers, "all in the same boat . . . each of them visibly

at sea. Yes, yes, these
old folks grown unpresuming,
almost Japanese,

had embarked too soon
—Bon voyage! Write!—upon their
final honeymoon.

Later he describes a visit to a Noh theater, where an actor plays the parts successively of a maiden pearl diver,
her mother's ghost, and a dancing dragon. The per-
former is

a middle-aged man—
but time, gender, self are laws
waived by his gold fan.

A diver, a benevolent ghost, and a dancing dragon—
that is how I want to remember him.

✴

To conjure spirits from the vasty deep of one's own
mind is always dangerous. But there are sometimes
reasons for doing so. Before he began to publish the
Ouija-board poems, Jimmy was a much-admired minor

writer, whose work had been called a poetry of surfaces, and was often described in words like "elegant," "sensitive," "erudite," "fluent," and "witty." Perhaps it was natural that he should have wanted more, that he should have hoped to create a long, serious poem, a major work that could stand next to those of Yeats, Auden, and Eliot. In the opinion of some critics he succeeded brilliantly. Sandy McClatchy, who is one of James Merrill's co-executors, has called *Sandover*

> —with the possible exception of Whitman's "Song of Myself"—the strangest and grandest American poem ever: at once eerie, hilarious, and heartbreaking.

I can agree with these last three adjectives, though not with the overall judgment.

Today I think that there may have been other, more generous and courageous motives besides literary ambition behind *Sandover*. Once the spirits had been contacted, to have refused their messages could have seemed cowardly, cautious, overrational. The Ouija-board project might have seemed a chance to remain close to David after their erotic connection was over. It might also have seemed a way to release David from his despair about the failure of his novels and allow him to collaborate on a major project. Later, it might have seemed a way to give Peter, whose theatrical career was going nowhere, the chance to become, for a few moments on stage or video, the incarnation of a god.

※

How much should one risk for art? What chances should one take? Should one seek productive derangements of the mind (by drugs, drink, sleeplessness, passion)? What about physically risky actions: climbing mountains, exploring jungles, driving too fast, associating with violent persons, traveling to dangerous places, seeking out wars, riots, and revolutions? Should one investigate risky ideas—form intense relationships with charismatic but possibly unreliable gurus, or with voices that may be those of demons? And what about using, or using up, not only your own life but also those of your friends and lovers?

If you take no chances, make no sacrifices, and reject the irrational in any form, how can you ever "make it new"? And if you decide to take these chances, will the end justify the means? Unfortunately, we cannot know the answer to any of these questions until long, long afterwards.

PERMISSIONS